Elvis Wellness

Elvis Wellness

BOOK OF ECCLESIASTES

Johnny A. Palmer Jr.

ISBN-13: 9780692704912
ISBN-10: 0692704914

Contents

Introduction

§

THERE YOU ARE. THE ROOM is filled with chatter, excitement, and anticipation. All of a sudden the lights slowly go out and silence fills the air. Then the sound of 2001 Space Odyssey begins. Finally out of nowhere comes Elvis – the sideburns, the shaky leg, and the sound of See See Rider fills the atmosphere. The music magic begins, let the good times roll! And for the next hour or so the sound of everything from Hound Dog to Suspicious Minds is in full swing, peppered with "Thank you, thank you, very much!" And before you know it that dreaded song, "Wise men say…" Dread because you know the concert is coming to an end. Elvis is rushed out into his, let's head for Graceland, limousine. The excitement comes to a crashing halt by the distinctive voice of <u>Al Dvorin</u>, *"Elvis has left the building. Thank you and good night."*

Elvis left the building permanently on August 16, 1977. Elvis was not God, just an entertainer, just a man and he knew it. Once during a concert in South Bend Indiana, Sept. 30, 1974 a fan held up a sign which read "Elvis is King." Elvis said, "I haven't been caught up ah in this thing, and I can't accept this kingship thing because to me there's only one – which is Christ." You can hear Elvis saying those words on YouTube.

But all of this reminds me of the true and living God, I can hear the 2001 Space Odyssey playing away as God says, "Let there be light!" God! What an awesome Being He really is! He is the One who created man and placed him in a beautiful garden. Generously giving Adam and Eve freely everything their hearts could possible desire, holding back only one tree with a very simple warning:

¹⁶ The LORD God commanded the man, saying, "From any tree of the garden you may eat freely; ¹⁷ but from the tree of the knowledge of good and evil you shall not eat, for in the day that you eat from it you will surely die." Genesis 2:16-17

Adam did eat, and as a result God left the buildings so to speak, I realize that God, being omnipresent, cannot in a sense leave or show up anywhere! And yet the Bible does speak of God's coming on the Day of Pentecost (Acts 2) and the Restrainer being removed at the rapture (2 Thess. 2). Now when someone receives the Lord Jesus Christ as their Savior, they are indwelt by God Himself (Jn. 1:12 with Gal. 4:6). But even after we are saved we have a choice of walking in the Spirit or according to the flesh (Gal. 5:16-17). Now when we live according to the flesh we lose not the indwelling presence of God, but His manifested presence (Jn. 14:21). You might want to get a copy of my book *Spiritual Survivor Man* to explore this concept more fully. So in a real sense it *seems* as if God has left the building. All of this leads me to a very unique book in the Bible, called Ecclesiastes. You may not be familiar with this book; you might have to look at the front of your Bible, under the table of content, to even find it. But believe me, it will be well worth the effort, so what do you say we dust it off and take a peek? It is a book that basically tells us what life is like after God, so to speak, leaves the building. Did I say life? It is not really life but mere existence, one that is barely tolerable and extremely empty. It is God alone who makes life worth living; this book is designed to convince us of that very simple yet tremendously important truth. I would suggest that we begin by reading the entire book of Ecclesiastes at least five times. I know, that seems like a lot to ask and to those unfamiliar with how to get the most out of God's Word, it may even appear to be a waste of time. Trust me on this one, we can never ever read God's Word too much, it's one for the money, two and it begins to show, three to get you ready, and soon it's go cat go! When we get into God's Word, and yes even this almost forgotten book is inspired Scripture, we will discover the Holy Spirit getting that buried treasure into our inner being.

CHAPTER 1

Didja' Ever

§

(*Word* about emptiness)

1 THESE ARE THE WORDS of the teacher, the son of David, king in Jerusalem. Teacher: 2 Life is fleeting, like a passing mist. It is like trying to catch hold of a breath; All vanishes like a vapor; everything is a great vanity. 3 What good does it do anyone to work so hard again and again, sun up to sundown? All his labor to gain but a little? [The Voice Bible: Step Into the Story of Scripture]

DIDJA' EVER

Didja' ever get
Didja' ever get one
Didja' ever get one of them
Didja' ever get one of them days, boy
Didja' ever get one of them days
When nothin' is right from mornin' till night
Didja' ever get one of them days
Didja' ever get one of them days
[From the movie G.I. Blues, 1960 sung by Elvis Presley]

It's one thing to have one of those days, but when one of those days turns into one of those life's we can say, "Houston we got us a big problem!" Life lived without the true and living God is bound to usher in such a life. The following words by William Shakespeare could have been written by King Solomon of old:

Tomorrow, and tomorrow and tomorrow
creeps in this petty pace from day to day,
To the last syllable of recorded time,
And all our yesterdays have lighted fools
The way to dusty death.

Out, Out, brief candle
Life's but a walking shadow, a poor player
That struts and frets his hour upon the stage
and then is heard no more. It is a tale
Told by an idiot. Full of sound and fury
SIGNIFYING NOTHING.
[Macbeth (Act 5, Scene 5, lines 17-28]

The question before us is, "Is life really worth living?" In essence Solomon concludes – "Not really! Not IF you leave God out of the picture. It is a tale told by an idiot signifying nothing."

The Subject of the book of Ecclesiastes – Vanity of Vanities, all is vanity! All is meaningless, pointless, emptiness, and useless. How utterly tragic when life becomes hollow and we feel unfulfilled, insignificant, useless, and just plain irrelevant. Listen to how the Message Bible puts it:

[1] These are the words of the Quester, David's son and king in Jerusalem: [2] Smoke, nothing but smoke. [That's what the Quester says.] There's nothing to anything— it's all smoke. [3] What's there to show for a lifetime of work, a lifetime of working your fingers to the bone? Ecclesiastes 1:1-3 (MSG)

THE *MAN* WHO WROTE THIS JOURNAL
HE IS A *SPEAKER*
The words of the Preacher - The root word means to assemble together. The implication is of one who spoke before an assembly of people.

"Preacher" is not the only way to translate the Hebrew name Qoheleth, we could use words like Teacher, the Philosopher, or Spokesman… Yet "Preacher" may be the best translation of all. The Hebrew root of the word qoheleth literally means "to gather, collect, or assemble." The verb qoheleth refers to the gathering or assembly of a community of people, especially for the worship of God. So Qoheleth is not so much a teacher in a classroom but more like a pastor in a church… "Ecclesiastes" is a form of the Greek word ekklesia, which is the common New Testament word for "church." An ekklesia is not a church building but a congregation— a gathering or assembly of people for the worship of God. The word "ecclesiastes" is the Greek translation of the Hebrew word qoheleth. Literally, it means "one who speaks in the ekklesia"— that is, in the assembly or congregation… "Preacher" is a very appropriate title for Solomon. He was the king, of course, yet when Solomon dedicated the temple in 1 Kings 8, the Bible says that he "assembled" Israel (v. 1), and then it repeatedly says that the Israelites formed an "assembly" (e.g., v. 14)." [EWEM]

He was a man of *Stature the son of David, king in Jerusalem*- the only son David had, that was king, was Solomon. The significance of this is that this man had the resources to search out every avenue of life. He had tried to find satisfaction in life through wine, women, wealth, worldliness, wisdom, works, and wickedness – and came up short - empty. His bucket not only had a hole in it, it had no bottom at all. And that is in spite of the fact that his bucket had dipped into every imagined stream that life had to offer. There is a familiar saying these days, "Been there, done that!" Meaning the thrill is gone. When I was in Nicaragua I went on the Zip line, it was exciting and scary and new. I asked a fellow believer who was part of our group, "Are you not going on the Zip line?" He said rather matter-factly, "No, I already been on it several times!" Just about anything and everything we can think of, things that should bring meaning and purpose to life – Solomon could say, "No big deal! I have been there and done that."

Elvis once said, "Those movies sure got me into a rut." Sometimes if honesty prevails I have to say, "This life sure got me into a rut!"

His *Motto*
The *Futility* of life

"Vanity of vanities," says the Preacher; "Vanity of vanities, all is vanity." - Solomon liked that word "vanity"; he used it 38 times in Ecclesiastes. The word means "emptiness, futility, vapor, that which vanishes quickly and leaves nothing behind."

There was a contest at a College for the students to give the best definitions of life. Here are some of those definitions:

* One college student wrote that, "Life is a joke that isn't even funny."
* Another wrote, "Life is a jail sentence we get for the crime of being born."
* Another said, "Life is a disease for which the only cure is death."
* Erma Bombeck once said, "If life is a bowl of cherries, why do I always get the pits?"

We try to pretend life is exciting and things are happening but if truth be known life is more routine and boring then action packed. Reminds me of something I read saying, "There have been many interesting stories written about the excitement that goes on in Suite 1102. They describe the time that Ed Sullivan had Ezio Pinza surprise Sylvia outside the door by singing "Some Enchanted Evening" and the afternoon Elvis Presley walked in the room while Mrs. Sullivan was playing cards with her friends. The anecdotes make good copy but are not typical of the atmosphere. It is so quiet and there are so few visitors that at least three of his secretaries have quit out of boredom (and he has only-had half a dozen)." [Harris, Michael (2010-12-07). Always On Sunday: An Inside View of Ed Sullivan, the Beatles, Elvis, Sinatra & Ed's Other Guests (Kindle Locations 173-175).]

"I hope I didn't bore you too much with my life story." Elvis Presley

Why is this? Because mankind was created by God and for God and since the Fall of mankind, human beings are separated from God. That separation was caused by a word that has all but fallen off the edge of the planet called –sin. I realize we are a "Whatever happen to sin" generation but that is what the real problem is – not climate change but defiant change in our hearts.

[20] For the creation was subjected to futility, not willingly, but because of Him who subjected *it* in hope; [21] because the creation itself also will be delivered from the bondage of corruption into the glorious liberty of the children of God. [22] For we know that the whole creation groans and labors with birth pangs together until now. Romans 8:20-22

Hunter S. Thompson, a journalist, committed suicide on February 16, 2005 in his home in Aspen, Colorado. Thompson often wrote for Rolling Stone Magazine. He left instructions that his ashes should be shot out of a cannon atop a 153-foot tower to the tune of Bob Dylan's "Mr. Tambourine Man." Thompson was 67 when he died, and his family and friends said that he was in pain from hip replacement surgery, back surgery, and a recently broken leg. He'd talked about suicide for more than 25 years. February 2005 was particularly grim month for him because football season was over. The brief suicide message scrawled with a black marker and titled "Football Season Is Over," reads as follows:

"No More Games. No More Bombs. No More Walking. No More Fun. No More Swimming. 67. That is 17 years past 50. 17 more than I needed or wanted. Boring. I am always [cranky]. No Fun—for anybody. 67. You are getting Greedy. Act your old age. Relax—This won't hurt." [Reuters, on AOL News (9-8-05); submitted by Lee Eclov, Vernon Hills, Illinois]

It is a Fact of life, *What profit has a man from all his labor In which he toils* –if you leave God and eternity out of the picture what real meaning does all of our work amount to?

For what will it profit a man if he gains the whole world, and loses his own soul?" Mark 8:36

Leonard Woolf author and publisher wrote, "I see clearly that I have achieved practically nothing. The world today and the history of the human ant hill during the past five to seven years would be exactly the same if I had played Ping-Pong instead of sitting on committees and writing books and memoranda. I have therefore to make a rather ignominious confession that I have in a long life ground through between 150,000 and 200,000 hours of perfectly useless work." [Leonard Woolf, author and publisher (Hogarth Press), literary editor of *The Nation. Wireless Age, Sept-Nov 1998, 35*]

The problem is, if we leave God out of the picture, we are going the wrong way! We are living with either the wrong purpose or no purpose at all! It reminds me of something, that happen many years ago, at the Rose Bowl in Pasadena. The University of California and Georgia Tech were doing battle. It was late in the second quarter. Thomason carrying the ball for Georgia Tech is hit, and he fumbles the ball. And, the center for California, Roy Regals picks it up, and starts toward the goal line. Only one thing wrong: He's gotten confused, and he's headed toward the wrong goal. Roy runs 67 yards toward the wrong goal with his teammates trying to tackle him and his opponents leading interference for him. Finally, he is stopped on the one-yard line, tackled by one of his own teammates. Can you imagine—running with the ball toward the wrong goal? I can!

That's the problem with everyone who leaves God and eternity out of their lives…They are confused, living with the wrong purpose or no purpose at all. Sound strange to me – purpose. Sounds like some sort of fish moving through the water. Purpose a life must have…

THE *MIND-SET*

under the sun – this is the key to understanding this book. The phrase is found 29 times and speaks of living life from a humanistic point of view. It is living life without including God and eternity in one's thinking. Only God can occupy the God-sized vacuum in every human heart. Nothing we do in the immediate can replace the fulfillment that comes from the Ultimate. Obviously the only thing that can give us eternal satisfaction is the Eternal One. Who but the Infinite God could possible give the finite ongoing and lasting fulfillment? Or as Augustine put it, " the soul is restless until it finds its rest in God." Dr. McCook imagines a conversation between a bird and a mole which has just pushed up its head out of the ground:

> He heard a bird singing up above on the branch of a tree. He asked the bird, "What are you making such a noise about?" The bird replied cheerfully, "O, the sunshine, the trees, the grasses, the shining stream yonder, and the white clouds on the mountain side. The world is full

of beauty." Mr. Mole said, "Nonsense! I have lived in this world longer than you have, and I have gone deeper into it. I have traversed it and tunneled it, and I know what I am talking about, and I tell you there is nothing in it but worms."

[Knight's Master book of New Illustrations, A bird and a Mole, p. 368]

Life confined to this life is mole living – there is nothing down here worth getting overly excited about. If all we have is "only this life" then life sucks, and deep down we know it!

And if being a Christian is of value to us only now in this life, we are the most miserable of creatures. 1 Corinthians 15:19 (TLB)

Peggy Noonan said it well, "I think we have lost the old knowledge that happiness is overrated—that, in a way, life is overrated. We have lost somehow a sense of mystery—about us, our purpose, our meaning, and our role. Our ancestors believed in two worlds, and understood this to be the solitary, poor, nasty, brutish and short one. We are the first generation of man that actually expected to find happiness here on earth, and our search for it has caused such unhappiness. The reason: if you do not believe in another, higher world, if you believe only in the flat material world around you, if you believe that this is your only chance at happiness—if that is what you believe, then you are more than disappointed when the world does not give you a good measure of its riches, you are in despair." [Peggy Noonan in Life, Liberty and the Pursuit of Happiness. Christianity Today, Vol. 38, no. 11.]

Life lived without keeping God and eternity in mind is a life doomed to be senseless and meaningless. Clarence Darrow was an American lawyer and leading member of the American Civil Liberties Union, best known for defending John T. Scopes in the Scopes "Monkey" Trial(1925), in which he opposed William Jennings Bryan. He was a very vocal atheist and was described candidly by one of his contemporaries, Harry Emerson Fosdick:

"To him the "outstanding fact" of human life is the utter "futility of it all"; he thinks that possibly "no life is of much value, and every death is little loss" to the world; he feels that the "most satisfactory part of life is the time spent in sleep, when one is utterly oblivious to existence" and "the next best is when one is so absorbed in activities like poker games" that one is altogether unmindful of self. Rapidly accumulating testimony bears witness that such futilism is one of irreligion's commonest effects. To argue from atheism to badness is false in both fact and theory, but to argue from atheism to depressed enthusiasm about living is plain sailing. The outstanding fact that cannot be dodged by thoughtful men is the futility of it all."

Anytime our lives become empty and without meaning we can be sure that we have lost our focus on God and eternity, when that happen we will be singing Didja' Ever get one of those lives boy! But when we keep our focus on God and eternity, life begins to take on real meaning. Not long ago I was discouraged about how fruitless and empty my ministry seemed. A book I enjoy reading by Watchman Nee, called The Normal Christian Life, helped put things into perspective:

"One day I was walking along the street with a stick, very weak and in broken health, and I met one of my old college professors... He looked at me from head to foot and from foot to head, and then he said: 'Now look here; during your college days we thought a good deal of you and we had hopes that you would achieve something great. Do you mean to tell me that this is what you are?" Nee writes, "My career, my health, everything had gone, and here was my old professor who taught me law in school, asking me: "Are you still in this condition, with no success, no progress, nothing to show?" But the very next moment – I really knew what it meant to have the "Spirit of glory" resting upon me...To my professor it seemed a total waste to serve the Lord; but that is what the Gospel is for – to bring us to a true estimate of His worth...If the Lord is worthy, then how can it be a waste? He is worthy to be served. He is worthy for me to be His prisoner. He is worthy for me just to live for. Has someone been telling you that you are wasting your life by sitting still and not doing much?... Then remember this, that He will never be satisfied without our "wasting" ourselves upon Him."

[The Normal Christian Life by Watchman Nee, pp. 187-188]

Heartbreak Hotel

§

(*Watching* Nature)

4 ONE GENERATION COMES, ANOTHER goes; but the earth continues to remain. 5 The sun rises and the sun sets, laboring to come up quickly to its place again and again. 6 The wind in its travels blows toward the south, then swings back around to the north. Back and forth, returning in its circuit again and again. 7 All rivers flow to the sea, but the sea is never full. To the place where the rivers flow, there the water returns to flow once again. 8 Words, words, words! So many words! They are wearisome things; and yet people cannot refrain from speaking. No eye has ever surveyed the world and said, "I have seen enough"; no ear has ever listened to creation and said, "I have heard enough." Eccles. 1:4-8

> Well, since my baby left me
> Well, I found a new place to dwell
> Well, it's down at the end of Lonely Street
> At Heartbreak Hotel
> Where I'll be--where I get so lonely, baby
> Well, I'm so lonely
> I get so lonely, I could die.
> [From Elvis' Golden Records, 1956]

His breakthrough hit was Heartbreak Hotel, released in 1956 - a song inspired by a newspaper article about a local suicide. When life is confined to under the sun living we feel like we have permanently checked into Heartbreak Hotel.

Life is so low and lonely we feel like we could die. We may look out our window and see a rainbow but deep inside we know that it's a chase that never ends. Judy Garland said it well:

> Why have I always been a failure?
> What can the reason be?
> I wonder if the world is to blame
> I wonder if it could be me
> I'm always chasing rainbows
> Watching clouds drifting by
> My schemes are just like all my dreams
> Ending in the sky
> Some fellas look and find the sunshine
> I always look and fine the rain
> Some fellas make a winning some time
> I never even make a gain
> Believe me
> I'm always chasing rainbows
> Waiting to find a little bluebird
> In vain

That is *under the sun* living! Keep in mind living "under the sun" is living life without being focused on God, in other words, this is what life is like when we view it from a merely human perspective. Last chapter we looked at the Subject of this book and now we begin to see the Sermons.

[4] A generation goes and a generation comes, But the earth remains forever. [5] Also, the sun rises and the sun sets; And hastening to its place it rises there *again.* [6] Blowing toward the south, Then turning toward the north, The wind continues swirling along; And on its circular courses the wind returns. [7] All the rivers flow into the sea, Yet the sea is not full. To the place where the rivers flow, There they flow again. [8] All things are wearisome; Man is not able to tell *it.* The eye is not satisfied with seeing, Nor is the ear filled with hearing. Ecclesiastes 1:4-8

THE *PERMANCY* OF THE EARTH

A generation goes and a generation comes, But the earth remains forever – this reminds us that our life is transitory and terribly brief. By the way, when someone dies we say "they passed away" here is where that phrase came from. In the overall scheme of things nature appears to be lasting while man is leaving, not long after he arrives. Man is like a brief visitor waiting for his transitory hospital bed. Have you noticed that life is lived between two hospitals? You check into one when you're born and before you know it, you're checking out permanently in another one. Two things appear close together – the brevity of life and the certainty of death. Everybody is coming and going but the earth remains the same. Our emptiness is illustrated by the songs we sing. Tennessee Ernie Ford put it in words we can all understand:

> "Sixteen tons and what do you get?
> Another day older and deeper in debt.
> Saint Peter don't you call me,
> cause I can't go.
> I owe my soul, to the company store."

But old man death does call, as Tennessee Ernie Ford himself, discovered years ago. And while we must go, the old company store just keeps right on going as if we never existed. Like my little puppy walking across the yard, his light foot prints are nowhere to be found. That lawn was here before little *Buddy* was part of our family, and will be there long after he is no more – not to mention his owners! As we look at this planet we do not sense it is grieving over our departure but continues its laborious and somewhat boring cycle seemingly accomplishing absolutely nothing. It all seems so twisted and distorted, why should a planet, that was made for human beings and that was created to bow before our dominion end up being so lasting and we so fragile.

When we were in Nicaragua they showed us the hotel where Howard Hughes was held up. Hughes was worth 2.5 billion at the time of his death. Think of it, all of that money and influence and yet he is gone and that very hotel where he stayed is still standing and doing fine! And what of Hughes who was at one time the richest man in the United States? Time Magazine wrote:

"Howard Hughes death was commemorated in Las Vegas by a minute of silence. Casinos fell silent. Housewives stood uncomfortable clutching their paper cups full of coins at the slot machines, the black jack games paused, and the crap tables with the stickmen cradled the dice in the crook of their wooden wands.

Then a pit boss looked at his watch, leaned forward and whispered, "Ok, roll the dice. He's had his minute."

As always, the Bible puts the cookies on the bottom shelf for all to partake of, and thus, become enlightened.

By the sweat of your face you will eat bread, till you return to the ground, because from it you were taken; For you are dust, And to dust you shall return." Genesis 3:19

Yet you do not know what your life will be like tomorrow. You are *just* a vapor that appears for a little while and then vanishes away. James 4:14

For, "ALL FLESH IS LIKE GRASS, AND ALL ITS GLORY LIKE THE FLOWER OF GRASS. THE GRASS WITHERS, AND THE FLOWER FALLS OFF, 1 Peter 1:24

Life is this tiny duration and then we die. Then what? I suppose the kids rummage through our stuff to see if any of it is worth hanging onto. There is not! We say our children are our future; they will be able to accomplish things that go beyond anything we could ever dream… But, as usual, Ecclesiastes takes a gloomier view. Soon the younger generation will become the older generation, and then there will be a generation after that. It is always the same… The rise of each generation gives the impression that something actually is happening, but nothing really is." [Ryken, Philip Graham (2010-04-08). Ecclesiastes: Why Everything Matters (Preaching the Word) (p. 26). Crossway. Kindle Edition.]

Jerome said, "What is more vain than this vanity: that the earth, which was made for humans, stays— but humans themselves, the lords of the earth, suddenly dissolve into the dust?"

Remember this is true only when we confine ourselves to under the sun living and leave God out of the picture. Ryken again notes, "The reason the Preacher shows us the weariness of our existence, making us more and more disillusioned with life under the sun, is so we will not expect to find meaning and satisfaction in earthly things, but only in God Himself. Some people think that Ecclesiastes is about the meaninglessness of human existence. This perspective is not quite correct, however. Ecclesiastes is really about the meaninglessness of life without God."

John Wesley noted, "Began expounding the Book of Ecclesiastes, never before had I so clear a sight either of its meaning or beauties. Neither did I imagine, that the several parts of it were in so exquisite a manner connected together, all tending to prove the grand truth, that there is no happiness out of God."

THE *PERPETUAL* MOTION OF THE SUN

The sun also rises, and the sun goes down, And hastens to the place where it arose – this highlights our sense of meaningless. As we watch the sun rise and set over and over again, we are reminded of our life. What does it really accomplish? Like the sun, after all of its relentless motion, the heavens remain the same! One day is just another carbon copy of another.

"Up in the morning, out on the job
Work like the devil for my pay.
While that lucky old sun, got nothing to do.
But roll around heaven all day."

"Truth is like the sun. You can shut it out for a time, but it ain't going away."
Elvis Presley

Nothing ever gets settled! We can never really say this is finished; that has now been permanently put to bed. Duane Thomas played football for the Dallas Cowboys, and went to the Super Bowl in 1972 with them. After they won, he was asked by a reporter, "How does it feel to win the big one?" He said, "If it's such a big game, why do they play another again next year?"

How many today are busy doing things that in light of eternity amount to absolutely nothing? Rafael Antonio Lozano is a man with a mission, albeit a strange one. The 33-year-old computer programmer from Plano, Texas, is on a quest to visit every company-owned Starbucks on the planet. Rafael, who calls himself Winter, began his mission in 1997, when there were 1,304 such stores worldwide. Today, there are over 6,000 in 37 countries. As of October 31st, 2005, Winter had visited 4,918 Starbucks in North America, in addition to 213 others around the globe. Despite his impressive pace, Winter is realistic about the nature of his quest, saying, "As long as they keep building Starbucks, I'll never be finished."

He is also realistic about the importance of his mission. "Every time I reach a Starbucks, I feel like I've accomplished something, when actually I've accomplished nothing." [Jayne Clark, "Sooner or Latte, He'll Get There," USAToday. com (10-13-05); submitted by Sam O'Neal, St. Charles, Illinois]

But in contrast when we live for Christ we are promised an eternal reward! That alone makes our brief stay worth the effort. Just to get a gulp of air in our despair, listen to the breath taking Word of God:

And without faith it is impossible to please *Him,* for he who comes to God must believe that He is and *that* He is a rewarder of those who seek Him. Hebrews 11:6

"Behold, I am coming quickly, and My reward *is* with Me, to render to every man according to what he has done.

Revelation 22:12

The *Perplexing* Wind

The wind goes toward the south, And turns around to the north; The wind whirls about continually, And comes again on its circuit – the wind is in constant motion, following "circuits" that man cannot fully understand or chart. Jesus said, "The wind blows where it wishes, and you... cannot tell where it comes from and where it goes" (John 3:8). The wind is constantly moving and changing directions – it does not appear to make sense. Just as we cannot understand the why's and wherefore's of the wind – we cannot make sense of our lives either. During the 2007-2008 NFL regular season, New England Patriots' quarterback Tom Brady set the record for most touchdown passes in a regular season, paving the way for his winning the MVP award. At the age of 30, he has already won three Super Bowls—an accomplishment that sets him apart as one of the best quarterbacks to ever play the game. In 2005, Tom Brady was interviewed by *60 Minutes* journalist Steve Kroft. Despite the fame and career accomplishments he had achieved already, Brady told Kroft that it felt like something was still lacking in his life:

"Why do I have three Super Bowl rings and still think there's something greater out there for me? I mean, maybe a lot of people would say, 'Hey man, this is what [it's all about].' I reached my goal, my dream, my life. Me?

I think, 'It's got to be more than this.' I mean this isn't—this can't be—all it's cracked up to be."

Kroft pressed Brady as to what the right answer was, and Brady added:

"What's the answer? I wish I knew... I love playing football, and I love being quarterback for this team. But at the same time, I think there are a lot of other parts about me that I'm trying to find." [Van Morris, Mount Washington, Kentucky; source: www.cbsnews.com and 60 Minutes (CBS, 2007)]

The only answer to be found is in God! As previously said, but bears repeating, we were created by God and for God. Only He can give us life abundantly.

The thief does not come except to steal, and to kill, and to destroy. I have come that they may have life, and that they may have *it* more abundantly. John 10:10

Jesus Christ offers an abundant life – a life that answers the questions of *Who* am I; *Where* did I come from; *Why* am I here; and *Where* am I going? But this is not realized by those who live only under the sun.

This book of Ecclesiastes is rarely understood because people misunderstand the point of this book. It is *not* a book showing you how to live life with God and eternity in mind! It is designed to show what happens when we don't. Those who are insecure and immature will quickly turn away from this book thinking that it is supporting such an empty life – it is not! It is simple showing us the inevitable results of leaving God and eternity out of the picture. We have to let the despair sink in before we can get the full value of this book. If we smuggle God into to this book before the feeling of emptiness without God sinks in, we miss the blessed point of how much we need God in our lives.

The *Purposeless* Rivers

All the rivers run into the sea, Yet the sea is not full; To the place from which the rivers come, There they return again — with all of its commotion and constant flowing what exactly does the flowing of the rivers really accomplish? No matter how many centuries the rivers flow they never fill up the Sea. Likewise no matter what we do, how hard we work at it, nothing is ever finished or accomplished in our brief lives.

> "I gets weary and filled with troubles,
> I'm tired of liv'en and feared of dying,
> But Old Man River he just keeps rollin
> along."

I have a treadmill in my house and I like to watch something on TV when I walk. So I walk and walk and walk — and then I get off, right where I started! Go figure. William McDonald describes such a life:

"Frail man's life is filled with labor and activity, but where does it get him when all is said and done? He is on a treadmill, a tiresome round of motion without progress. You ask him why he works, and he replies, "To get money, of course." But why does he want money? To buy food. And why does he want food? To maintain his strength. Yes, but why does he want strength? He wants strength so he can work. And so there he is, right back where he began." Four psychologists did a study of notable quotations from famous people around the world about the meaning of life. The study analyzed the quotes of 195 men and women who lived within the past few hundred years. Here's a summary of the major themes and some of the people representing each theme:

* *Life is primarily to be enjoyed and experienced. Enjoy the moment and the journey.* 17 percent of the famous people in the study endorsed this theme (Ralph Waldo Emerson, Cary Grant, Janis Joplin, and Sinclair Lewis). Janis Joplin is best known for her lyric: "You got to get it while you can." The problem is without Christ you cannot really enjoy life; and when life ends what do you do?

- *We live to express compassion to others, to love; to serve.*13 percent endorsed this theme (Albert Einstein, Mohandas Gandhi, and the Dalai Lama). Albert Einstein stated: "Only a life lived for others is a life worthwhile." But can we really love others without God's love flowing through us to others? Are sinful self-centered human being really worthy giving our lives for?

- *Life is unknowable; a mystery.*13 percent endorsed this theme (Albert Camus, Bob Dylan, and Stephen Hawking). Hawking wrote, "If we find an answer to that (why we and the universe exist), it would be the ultimate triumph of human reason—for then we would know the mind of God." While it's true life is a mystery and there are many things we cannot know – we can know the God who knows it all!

- *Life has no meaning.* 11 percent endorsed this (novelist Joseph Conrad, Sigmund Freud, Franz Kafka, Bertrand Russell, Jean Paul Sartre, and Clarence Darrow). Darrow compared life to a ship that is "tossed by every wave and by every wind; a ship headed to no port and no harbor, with no rudder, no compass, no pilot, simply floating for a time, then lost in the waves." But if we trust Christ as our Savior life can have meaning and purpose.

- *We are to worship God and prepare for the afterlife.* 11 percent endorsed this theme (Desmond Tutu, Billy Graham, Martin Luther King Jr., and Mother Teresa). Desmond Tutu said, "[We should] give God glory by reflecting his beauty and his love. That is why we are here, and that is the purpose of our lives." And that is reality!

- *Life is a struggle.* 8 percent endorsed this theme (Charles Dickens, Benjamin Disraeli, and Jonathan Swift). Swift wrote that life is a "tragedy wherein we sit as spectators for awhile and then act our part in it." Life is a struggle but we can trust the one who has been victorious over lives struggles!

- *We are to create our own meaning of life.* 5 percent endorsed this theme (Carl Sagan, Simone DeBeauvoir, and Carl Jung). Carl Sagan wrote: "We live in a vast and awesome universe in which, daily, suns are made and worlds destroyed, where humanity clings to an obscure clod of rock. The significance of our lives and our fragile realm derives from our own wisdom and courage. We are the custodians of life's meaning." Truth is only God can create! Whether it's physical life or meaning in life, it comes only from God's hand.

* *Life is a joke.* 4 percent endorsed this theme (Albert Camus, Charlie Chaplin, Lou Reed, and Oscar Wilde). Charlie
  Chaplin described life as "a tragedy when seen in close-up but a comedy in

* the long shot." The rock star Lou Reed said "Life is like Sanskrit read to a pony." Life is no joke especially for those who are under God's wrath...

[Richard Kinnier, Jerry Kernes, Nancy Tribbensee, Christina Van Puymbroeck; The Journal of Humanistic Psychology (Winter 2003); submitted by Jerry De Luca, Montreal West, Canada]

THE MAIN *POINT* WE LEARN FROM NATURE

All things are full of labor; Man cannot express it. The eye is not satisfied with seeing, Nor the ear filled with hearing – life under the sun never satisfies us. We all have sung Mick Jagger's song in our heart – "I can't get no satisfaction!" You might be thinking, "I know lost people who are happy and satisfied." I can assure you that their happiness is only temporary and outwardly – many people have a false satisfaction, a sort of suck it up mentality that will last only so long. In an early scene from the movie *Antz*, the main character, an ant named Z, lies on a leaf couch and tells his therapist:

"All my life I've lived and worked in the big city.... I always tell myself there has got to be something better out there. Maybe I, maybe I think too much. I think everything must go back to the fact that I had a very anxious childhood. My mother never had time for me. When you're the middle child in a family of 5 million, you don't get any attention.

I mean, how is it possible? I've always had these abandonment issues, which plagued me. My father was basically a drone, like I've said. The guy flew away when I was just a larva. And, my job, don't get me started on it because it really annoys me. I was not cut out to be a worker. I, I feel physically inadequate. My whole life I've never been able to lift more than ten times my own bodyweight. And, and, when you get down to it, handling dirt is not my idea of a rewarding career....I mean, what is it, I'm supposed to do everything for the colony? What about my needs? What about me? I mean I've got to believe there's some place out there that's better than this. Otherwise I'll just curl up into a larva position and weep. The whole system makes me feel...insignificant." The therapist responds, "Excellent! You've made a real breakthrough!"

Z says, "I have?" The therapist says, "Yes, Z. You *are* insignificant!" As Z goes to his workstation, he says to himself, "OK, I've just got to keep a positive attitude. A good attitude—even though I'm utterly insignificant. I'm insignificant, but with attitude."

[Antz *(Dreamworks, 1998), rated PG, written by Todd Alcott, Chris and Paul Weitz, directed by Eric Darnell and Tim Johnson V.; submitted by Jerry De Luca, Montreal West, Quebec*]

Many who have rejected God – have done it with an attitude! But the longer they live and the older they get, they will most certainly be faced with reality. You don't have to observe the monotony of nature very long before you're ready to check into Heartbreak Hotel. And as for chasing those rainbows it always seems to be in vain. On June 22, 1969, the headlines read – "Judy has found the end of the rainbow." The article read:

"Judy Garland has been found dead in her London apartment. She was 47 years old. While suicide is not yet proven, it is known that she tried to take her life 20 times before. Why would such a talented woman despise herself? Her devoted fans do not know, they always showered her with loving applause.

Judy was born Frances Gumm in Grand Rapids Michigan. Judy went from a family stage act to a film star at the age of 13 [Wizard of Oz]. She wed 5 times and had 3 children. Pills to settle her nerves and seesawing weight left her a shadow with a marvelous voice."

If she would have received the Lord Jesus Christ as Savior and become a God chaser – then at death she would have found the rainbow that she had been chasing all of her life.

Elvis said, "Man that record came out and was real big in Memphis. They started playing it, and it got real big. Don't know why -the lyrics had no meaning." [Kirov, Blago (2014-02-09). Elvis Presley: Quotes & Facts (p. 29). Blago Kirov. Kindle Edition]

CHAPTER 3

Follow that Dream

§

(Nothing new in the *Whole* of history)

9 WHAT HAS BEEN, THAT will be; what has been done, that will be done. Nothing is new under the sun; the future only repeats the past. 10 One person may say of some idea, "Pay attention to this; it's original!" But that same idea has already been expressed; it's been with us through the ages. 11 We do not remember those people and events of long ago, as future generations will not remember what is yet to come. Eccles. 1:9-11

> I've got to follow that dream wherever that dream may lead
> I've got to follow that dream to find the love I need
> When your heart gets restless, time to move along
> When your heart gets weary, time to sing a song
> But when a dream is calling you,
> There's just one thing that you can do
> Well, you gotta follow that dream wherever that dream may lead
> You gotta follow that dream to find the love
>
> you need Keep a-movin', move along, keep a moving...
> [From the movie Follow that Dream, 1961]

Yea we follow that dream, we get restless and weary and keep a-movin, move along but when do we ever catch it! We follow our dreams so long they become stale reruns, like watching a bad movie that we have seen too many times. How

21

about something new! In the last century, Lord Kelvin, a physicist and president of Britain's prestigious Royal Society, stated that "radio has no future." He also contended that "heavier-than-air flying machines are impossible" and that "X-rays will prove to be a hoax." About the same time, a British parliamentary committee dismissed Thomas Edison's incandescent lamp as "unworthy of attention of practical or scientific men." In 1889 the director of the United States Patent Office urged President William McKinley to close down the office because "everything that can be invented has been invented." [6000 Plus Illustrations for Communicating Biblical Truths, Old Age, Famous Future Failures]. Man loves to find new things, new dreams, and we laugh at people who say there is nothing new to be discovered. We are all like that bunch Paul addressed at Mars Hill.

For all the Athenians and the foreigners who were there spent their time in nothing else but either to tell or to hear some new thing. Acts 17:21

And yet Solomon makes a bold assertion that there is really nothing new under the sun. The dream you're following is not only unattainable but it's about as fresh as last month's TV Guide! We have seen the vanity from Watching nature; now the vanity of nothing being new in the Whole of history.

[9] What was will be again, what happened will happen again. There's nothing new on this earth. Year after year it's the same old thing. [10] Does someone call out, "Hey, *this* is new"? Don't get excited—it's the same old story. [11] Nobody remembers what happened yesterday. And the things that will happen tomorrow? Nobody'll remember them either. Don't count on being remembered. Ecclesiastes 1:9-11 (MSG)

LIFE IS *CONTINUOUS* OF WHAT HAS BEEN
The Present is a repeat of the Past

That which has been is what will be – he is saying the present is merely a repeat of the past. Rudyard Kipling had it right:

"The craft that we call modern;
The crimes that we call new;
John Bunyan had them typed,
And filed in 1692."

J. Vernon McGee gives this home spun background, "My grandfather courted my grandmother on an old horse-hair sofa. He proposed and she accepted. My dad courted my mother on a train, and they were married. I proposed to my wife sitting in a car. My grandson may propose to his wife in an airplane or maybe in a space capsule. You may ask, "Isn't that new?" The feeling that my grandfather had when his proposal was accepted was the same feeling I had, and I don't think my little grandson will feel any different. It is said the atomic bomb is new, but the atom had been around [since creation]. Well isn't the computer new?

Not really. God created us with computer brains and an electric system." [Thru the Bible Volumes 1-5 by J. Vernon McGee, Ecclesiastes]

It's like the beaver who told the rabbit as they stared up at the immense wall of Hoover Dam, "No, I didn't actually build it myself. But it was based on an idea of mine." There nothing really new going on, "...all things continue as *they were* from the beginning of creation." 2 Peter 3:4 (NKJV)

As Adrian Rogers noted, "Really, in spite of man's inventions and his so-called progress, it's just the cycle. We've just invented new ways to be mean, new ways to be wicked. We can get there faster, but we still don't know where we're going. History is like a broken phonograph record. It just keeps repeating itself. The answer is not in history." [The Adrian Rogers Legacy Collection, Ecclesiastes, The Perplexing Riddles of Life]

The Present will be repeated in the Future

That which is done is what will be done – everything we are doing today will be repeated in the future. Therefore in the grand scheme of things we are irrelevant – about to be replaced or retired at a moment's notice. During the contract negotiations some years ago between David Letterman and CBS, the possibility of Letterman signing on with ABC to replace Ted Koppel's "Nightline" was widely publicized. Some suggested that Ted Koppel's news program was no longer relevant. Ted Koppel made his feelings known regarding the situation. A *Washington Post* article quotes Koppel as saying:

"It is, at best, inappropriate and, at worst, malicious to describe what my colleagues and I are doing as lacking relevance." One ABC staffer was quoted as saying, "The hurtful part of it is being told you're not relevant anymore." Truth is whatever you are doing; someone else will be doing the same thing in the not too distant future…Such an aimless existence leads to despair! To think that everything we are doing, has been done before; and everything we are doing will be done again sort of kills the significance of what we are doing! The following are the last words spoken by famous individuals:

* "Nothing matters. Nothing matters."
  —*Louis B. Mayer, film producer; died October 29, 1957*
* "I'm bored with it all."
  —*Winston Churchill, statesman; died January 24, 1965*
  (Before slipping into a coma. He died 9 days later.)
* "Am I dying, or is this my birthday?"
  —*Lady Nancy Astor; died 1964*
  (When she woke briefly during her last illness and found all her family around her.)
* "Don't let me die; I have got so much to do."
  —*Huey Long, "The Kingfish," governor of and senator from Louisiana; died 1935*
* Following Elvis mother's death in 1957, he never watched the film "Loving You", again. [Kirov, Blago (2014-02-09). Elvis Presley: Quotes & Facts (p. 11). Blago Kirov. Kindle Edition]
* "My work is done. Why wait?"
  —*George Eastman, inventor; died 1932 (from his suicide note)*

Reminds me of the movie *Pinocchio*. It's about an Italian woodcarver who creates a boy puppet named Pinocchio. When a fairy magically gives the puppet life, Geppetto is obviously startled by what he sees in his shop.

The first conversation the old woodcarver has when he meets Pinocchio for the first time leads to a difficult question from the puppet-turned-real-"live"-boy. He looks at Pinocchio and asks, "Who are you?" "Well, you should know," Pinocchio replies. "You gave me my name." "Pi … Pi … Pi …" as he struggles to say the boy's name, still shocked by what has happened. Pinocchio shouts, "… nocchio!" Geppetto asks. "No. No. No. This can't be!" The old woodcarver is overwhelmed. He feels Pinocchio's arms and face to see if he is indeed a real "live" boy. Soon tears well up in his eyes. "You're alive! Do you understand? You're alive!" Pinocchio happily repeats his verdict: "I'm alive!" Then a pensive look comes over the face of the puppet-turned-boy. "What do you mean 'I'm alive'?" The woodcarver says, "What does it mean? Well, unless I'm going mad, and this isn't just a dream, it means you have a life to live," Pinocchio persists, "And what do you have a life for?" Geppetto falls silent, unable to find an answer. He concludes, "I'll have to think about it." If we leave God out of the picture we do not have a satisfactory answer to that question.

LIFE IS *CONSISTENT* WITH WHAT HAS BEEN

And there is nothing new under the sun. [10] *Is there anything of which it may be said, "See, this is new"? It has already been in ancient times before us* — someone says, "Was it not new putting a man on the moon?" Not really! What was new? Man was not new; the moon was not new; and making a discovery was not new. Man cannot "create" anything new because man is a mere creature, not the Creator! Only God can create new things, all man can do is take things that already exist and move them around. Henry Morris a Christian scientist notes:

"Verse 9 implies another great scientific principle, that of conservation of mass and energy. Nothing is now being either created or annihilated, everything is "conserved" and "there is no new thing under the sun." This fact is the most basic and best-proved law of science, finally demonstrated in the 19th century, but implied at many places in the Bible (note Gen. 2:1-3; Heb. 1:3; etc.). Matter may go through changes in state or form, and energy can be transformed from one kind of energy to another, but the totality of mass/energy (mass and energy are themselves inter-convertible under certain conditions) remains unchanged. Since everything in the physical word is either matter or energy, nothing is really new." [Morris, Henry M. (2001-07-31). The Remarkable Wisdom of Solomon (Kindle Locations 4024-4030). Master Books. Kindle Edition]

* God alone can create "new creatures":

[17] Therefore, if anyone *is* in Christ, *he is* a new creation; old things have passed away; behold, all things have become new. 2 Corinthians 5:17

⚬ God alone can enable one to walk "in newness of life":

[4] Therefore we were buried with Him through baptism into death, that just as Christ was raised from the dead by the glory of the Father, even so we also should walk in newness of life. Romans 6:4

⚬ God alone can give a new song:

[3] He has put a new song in my mouth-- Praise to our God; Many will see *it* and fear, And will trust in the LORD. Psalm 40:3

⚬ God alone allows the believer to enter by a new way:

[20] by a new and living way which He consecrated for us, through the veil, that is, His flesh, Hebrews 10:20

⚬ Only God can create "a new heaven and a new earth":

[1] Now I saw a new heaven and a new earth, for the first heaven and the first earth had passed away. Also there was no more sea. Revelation 21:1

⚬ Only God can make all things new:

[5] Then He who sat on the throne said, "Behold, I make all things new." And He said to me, "Write, for these words are true and faithful." Revelation 21:5

But nothing we do is really new. I always try to put together new and fresh sermons. I prepared new sermons for the Pastors in Nicaragua – but in reality there was nothing really new about them! The principles that I shared with them have been around for many years. Warren Wiersbe said, "A young man approached me at a conference and asked if he could share some new ideas for youth ministry. He was very enthusiastic as he outlined his program, but the longer I listened, the more familiar his ideas became. I encouraged him to put his ideas into practice, but then told him that we had done all of those things in Youth for Christ before he was born, and that YFC workers were still doing them. He was a bit stunned to discover that there was indeed nothing new under the sun." [Bible Expository Commentary (Be series), Ecclesiastes, Why we think things are new, by Warren Wiersbe]

The cults are nothing more than a rehash of what has been. You want to be a pantheist? Welcome to India. They were doing it in 2000 B.C. Or, if astral projection, is more your speed? Again, the Indians have been experts in that for centuries. How about Wiccan practices like the worship of mother earth? The Celts were doing it in A.D. 1400. There is nothing new that hasn't been tried before. This makes our contributions Frivolous. What real contributions can we make if everything has basically been done before? James Dobson had a friend who died unexpectedly; one of his colleagues gave a 5 minute eulogy and called for a one minute period of silence.

Then it was onto business as usual. He writes:

"I was thinking, "Lord, is this what it all comes down to? We sweat and worry and labor to achieve a place in life, to impress our fellow men. We take ourselves so seriously, overreacting to the insignificant events of each passing day. Then finally even for the brightest among us, all these experiences fade into history and our lives are summarized with a 5 minute eulogy and sixty seconds of silence. It hardly seems worth the effort."

And it's not – if we leave God and eternity out of the picture.

Man Is Not *Conscious* Of The Repetition

There is no remembrance of former *things,* nor will there be any remembrance of *things* that are to come by *those* who will come after – man has a poor memory! This makes our contributions sure to be Forgotten – as one noted, "Time blots out a multitude of events, as if they had never been. Men, as well as events, have passed away. How little is the remembrance of the great empire of Nimrod; of the earth beginnings of Rome; or the first dynasty of France? The heroes of the world – the mighty and illustrious, with all their titles and grandeur, pass away and are forgotten."

Back in 1978 one of two billionaires died in America. At the time his death was highly publicized. The paper wrote:

"A ministers son and an 8th grade dropout, he built one of the nation's largest fortunes by selling dollar-a-month insurance policies door to door, creating the

Bankers Life and Casualty from scratch during the Depression. His vast holdings included banks, textiles, oil, and Real Estate. Most of his wealth goes to charity and public service foundations." [Wikipedia.org. John D. MacArthur].

Surely everybody must remember such a wealthy and successful person? But how many of us know his name? I know now because I looked it up! Truth is we all sooner or later end up like Chuck Yeager, who said at his retirement, "I spent my life flying and there wasn't even a pigeon in the air when I said good-bye!" [Ecclesiastes The Mid-Life Crisis, by Don Anderson, p.40]

The Vanity of life is seen in the fact that there is nothing new in the Whole of history. If you leave God out of the picture, all of human history boils down to nothing but vanity…that also includes our personal history. The mighty Roman Empire fell and is a not even a passing thought to most people today. I read while excavating Roman ruins, archaeologists kept coming across the inscription "NFFNSNC." The inscriptions began appearing on grave markers in the first century and it continued through the last days of the empire. For the longest time, archeologists were stumped in its meaning. Then it came to light that NFFNSNC stood for the Roman proverb "Non Fui Fui Non Sum Non Curo" which means "I was not, I was, I am not, I do not care." [Preaching Illustrations Vol. 1 by Peter Kennedy, The emptiness of Rationalism p. 515]

Elvis once said, "Do something worth remembering" but that is easier said than done. But then he really did it!

CHAPTER 4

Wisdom of the Ages

§

(Human Wisdom)

Listen, to the wisdom of the ages
Listen, to the words of many sages

Live each day, as if it were your last
It's written in the stars, your destiny is cast
And that hourglass, runs too fast no doubt
For the sands of time are running out

Listen, to the wisdom of the ages
These words, can be found in history's pages.
[From the movie, Harum Scarum]

LISTEN TO THE WISDOM OF the ages – not! You can read sage after sage and walk away with your spiritual gas tank on empty. Even good old Alfie couldn't tell us what life was all about, remember him? I'll bet you would if you heard these words sung:

What's it all about, Alfie?
Is it just for the moment we live?
What's it all about when you sort it out,
Alfie?

Solomon is asking the same question – and he concludes that if it's all about human wisdom then it's all about being frustrated and grieved. All human wisdom brings is more soap bubbles!

[12] I, the teacher, was king over Israel in Jerusalem. [13]I decided to seek out and study the wisdom of the ages, of all that had been done under the heavens. I soon discovered the harsh realities of the work God has given us that keeps us so busy. [14]I have witnessed all that is done under the sun, and indeed, all is fleeting, like trying to embrace the wind.

[15]There is an old saying: Something crooked cannot be made straight, and something missing cannot be counted. [16]I mused over it all and thought to myself, "I have done great things, and I have gained more wisdom than anyone who reigned over Jerusalem before me. I have contemplated great wisdom and knowledge." [17]I decided to study wisdom and instead acquainted myself with madness and folly. It, too, seemed like trying to pursue the wind, [18]for as my wisdom increased, so did my vexation. As my knowledge grew, so did my pain. [Nelson, Thomas (2012-04-10). The Voice Bible: Step Into the Story of Scripture (p. 771). Thomas Nelson. Kindle Edition]

Now the wisdom Solomon is talking about in context is not the wisdom of God and His Word; it is wisdom derived from exploring human knowledge—philosophy, psychology, and logic — speaking of the best ideas that man can come up with or discover. He realizes that after all has been said and done, the educated man dies an educated failure. Because all the learning in the world cannot change the human heart or solve the real problems of life.

Human Wisdom Doesn't Bring Satisfacton Even To A Great Governor

I, the Preacher, was king over Israel in Jerusalem – Solomon was a great king over a great nation. He was the Donald Trump with much more ump! In the political realm he made Regan look like a political beginner, his economy made the United States look like a mom and pop operation. He was an addicted builder with more projects going then habitat for humanity. His clout stretched out politically, economically, and militarily. Yet, all of his exploits left him as empty as a Baptist preacher's wallet. This should convince us of politics — we think today that if we could just find another Ronald Regan, one who could brings in an economic boom with prosperity for everyone, we would be satisfied. Solomon, had all of that, but had to conclude that neither he nor the people were fulfilled. You can feel the frustration from both the President and the Congress, not to mention us Americans, over all of the problems, we are facing these days. Just take one example, look at all of these school shootings. They can hold hearings; ban every gun on the planet; and condemn the violence but they cannot stop the loss of life! To try and govern by human wisdom is futile because it cannot change people's hearts. In the movie *Mosquito Coast,* Harrison Ford plays an atheist who flees America to set up a perfect community in a remote jungle. Early in the movie, he meets a missionary (portrayed in the worst light possible) bound for the same area. When he arrives, the atheist sees immediate success in establishing a thriving village. But by the end of the movie, the atheist totally destroys his village because he finds out that even though he can help people scientifically, he cannot deal with their sinful hearts. And he also finds that he can't deal with his own sin. Meanwhile the unflatteringly portrayed missionary has a loyal, loving following of people at the end of the movie. Those people are joyful, hopeful, changed, and peaceful—a fact that irritates the atheist. He finally gets so enraged that he destroys everything around him and himself. [A Life Well Lived A Study of the Book of Ecclesiastes by Tommy Nelson p. 24]

HUMAN WISDOM DOESN'T *GAIN* MEANING IN LIFE
HIS PURSUIT
And I set my heart to seek and search out by wisdom - This was not a hobby or side interest for Solomon. It was the most important thing in his life at the time. He did not pursue this study of *human achievements* halfheartedly but fully committed himself to it.

In movie *Taken*, Bryan Mills, a former CIA operative who determines to track down his teenage daughter after she's been kidnapped by human traffickers while on a trip with a girlfriend in France. In one gripping scene, he tells one of the abductors:

"I don't know who you are. I don't know what you want…I can tell you I don't have money; but, what I do have are a very particular set of skills, skills that I've acquired over a very long career, skills that make me a nightmare for people like you. If you let my daughter go now, that will be the end of it. I will not look for you. I will not pursue you. But if you don't, I will look for you, I *will* find you and I *will* kill you." The abductor coolly replies: "Good luck." Bryan begins his relentless pursuit. He finally finds his daughter on a yacht, sold as a prostitute for a wealthy Arab businessman. Bryan is bloody and beaten but finds his daughter. Solomon is like that in his pursuit for the meaning of life – but he is living in the real world, which is not like the movies! [Elaine Larson, Addison, Illinois; source: Taken, Directed by Pierre Morel (Paris, France: EuoraCorp, 2008), DVD.]

Reminds me of the song "Here in the Real World" by Allan Jackson:

Cowboys don't cry,
And heroes don't die.
And good always wins
Again and again.

And love is a sweet dream
That always comes true
Oh, if life were like the movies,
I'd never be blue.

But here in the real world,
It's not that easy at all,
'Cause when hearts get broken,
It's real tears that fall.
And darlin', it's sad but true,
But the one thing I've learned from you,
Is how the boy don't always get the girl,
Here in the real world.

Solomon ends up bloodied and bruised, but all he finds is nothing but emptiness! And in the real world if we leave God and eternity out of the picture we end up with nothing but a blank canvas.

concerning all that is done under heaven — again leaving God and eternity out of the picture is what it means to limit our perspective to under heaven mind-set.

G. Campbell Morgan summarizes Solomon's outlook: "This man had been living through all these experiences under the sun, concerned with nothing above the sun... until there came a moment in which he had seen the whole of life. And there was something over the sun. It is only as a man takes account of that which is over the sun as well as that which is under the sun that things under the sun are seen in their true light." His Perplexity *this burdensome task God has given to the sons of man, by which they may be exercised. [14] I have seen all the works that are done under the sun; and indeed, all is vanity and grasping for the wind* - I read about a man named Floyd Collins, back in 1925, he was exploring a Cave in Kentucky and got stuck. He was 55 feet from the surface, the rescuers came but couldn't get him out. He was able to see the light; able to see where he wanted to be; but he was stuck and he couldn't get out. The newspapers got in on it, and thousands of people came to see him. They even sold hot dogs and sandwiches. It became a side show. Seventeen days later Floyd Collins died in that hole, able to see where he wanted to be but not able to get there. [Roger Thompson, "The Good News Is: The Bad News Is Wrong," Preaching Today, Tape No. 55.]. That's the way every person who lives by mere human wisdom ends up!

HUMAN WISDOM DOESN'T DO ANY *GOOD*

What is crooked cannot be made straight — he finds things that are wrong, things that are crooked and he cannot make those things right. Human wisdom always wants to straighten things out. Listen to these words of real wisdom:

* Physically, it lies upon the surface. We have no power to change one hair of our heads, or alter our statue (Mt. 5:36; 6:27).
* Intellectually, man's wisdom can never discover, much less remove, the causes of his restless misery.
* Spiritually, every faculty of man is under the perversity of the fall, and we have no more power to make straight its crookedness than to restore the whole work of God to its original uprightness."

And what is lacking cannot be numbered — it's like going through the drive through at one of these fast food joints. You order 3 burgers, 2 fries, and 2 cokes — but you cannot count 3 burgers because they only put in 2 burgers! But when you get home and open up the bag you cannot count that which is not there! Our human wisdom cannot change things!

In fact instead of changing a sick world, if we're not careful, it changes us and we become part of the problem rather than the solution. I read a book that recounts the stories of investigator Dan Walker's ministry to infiltrate brothels and free young women and children trapped in sex trafficking. Take a read:

"The adrenaline that pulsed through my veins during a rescue operation was more powerful and addictive than any extreme sport or self-induced high. The thrill … and the deep satisfaction that came with seeing a victim walk free from bondage and fear was exhilarating, and I had never been so alive. It should come as no surprise, then, that as time passed and I completed more missions, I started to change. This was not noticeable to me at the time, and I was only dimly aware of a growing distance between me and those around me...Having witnessed firsthand the horror of the sex trade and knowing how relatively easy it was to do something about it, I became even more eager to return to the front lines and rescue those I knew were still enslaved. In some cases the names and the faces of the victims began to haunt me, and I increasingly felt the burden of responsibility to go back for them...I began to feel the weight of the world on my shoulders and even came to believe that if I were not successful in my missions, then the victims concerned would never be rescued. If I did not go back for them, they would remain there forever." [Daniel Walker, <u>God in Brothel</u> (InterVarsity Press, 2011), pp. 118-119]

Did Dan end the sex trade? No, eventually Dan had a moral failure and his hopes of changing the world came to an abrupt end.

FIFTHLY, HUMAN WISDOM MAY BE *GREAT*

[16] *I communed with my heart, saying, "Look, I have attained greatness, and have gained more wisdom than all who were before me in Jerusalem. My heart has understood great wisdom and knowledge."* [17] *And I set my heart to know wisdom and to know madness and*

folly. I perceived that this also is grasping for the wind – none had greater wisdom than Solomon. The Point is that if human wisdom was the answer then Solomon would have found the answer in human wisdom! If a man with such great wisdom could not find satisfaction in human wisdom what makes us think we will find satisfaction with our lesser wisdom? The problem is, great human wisdom is void of divine wisdom! In one of the popular ads that accompanied the 2010 Super Bowl, Cars.com tells the fictional story of a wonder child named Timothy Richman. From his earliest years, Timothy displayed an amazing level of confidence, and his confidence came from knowledge. As a toddler eating in his high chair, he saw a pan of food cooking on the stove catch fire. Knowing somehow that baking soda puts out fires, Timothy calmly threw his rattle at a box of baking soda located on a shelf above the flaming pan, knocking over the box, which poured the soda into the pan and extinguished the flames. As a boy about to learn to ride a bike, Timothy stands straddling the bike as his dad prepares to put on the training wheels. Timothy says, "Balance, momentum, and a low center of gravity," and with that knowledge fully absorbed, before Timothy's dad can get the training wheels on, Timothy pedals the bike away and down the driveway. In junior high, Timothy confidently walks up to a teen on an Italian beach who has been stung on the leg by a jellyfish and acting on his knowledge of first aid he pours vinegar on the inflamed skin. He explains in perfect Italian that vinegar can neutralize jellyfish stings.

As a high school student on safari in Africa, he uses his knowledge of veterinary obstetrics to deliver a baby Bengal tiger that was breeched. As an adult, Timothy gets out of his car on a highway as a tornado approaches a bus full of cheerleaders. Using his knowledge of storm cells and tornadoes, he explains to the cheerleaders that they will be safe if they exit the bus and lie in a low-lying depression beside the road. Just as the cheerleaders and Timothy jump safely into the ditch, the bus rises in the air and is carried away by the tornado. But then Timothy stands with a frighten look on his face in a new car lot, It says "When it came time to buy a new car, he was just as nervous as the rest of us." Then Timothy sees a Cars.com sign and pulls out his cell phone. The narrator concludes, "So Timothy Richman got his knowledge at Cars.com, regained his confidence, and got the perfect car at the perfect price."[Craig Brian Larson, Editor of PreachingToday.com; source: 2010 USA Today Ad Meter and Cars.com].

This little commercial entertainingly illustrates the fact that no matter how much wisdom one has in one area of life, it does one no good in another area of life. One with human wisdom may be able to figure out a lot of things in this life; but when it comes to the meaning of life, such a one stands clueless as to how to find it! Apart from God and His wisdom man is clueless about the meaning of life regardless of how much human wisdom he has.

HUMAN WISDOM BRINGS MUCH *GRIEF*

[18] *For in much wisdom is much grief, And he who increases knowledge increases sorrow —* what does Solomon learn from his vast store of human wisdom and knowledge? He learns a proverb — "much wisdom brings much grief!" Reminds me of the comedian and actor Woody Allen. You would think he would be a laugh a minute. But one who interviewed him said:

"The funny thing about meeting Woody Allen is that he doesn't even try to make you laugh. Instead of an uproarious stream of one-liners, America's premier comedy director is more apt to launch into a thoughtful discourse on the senselessness of human existence."

Woody Allen: "In real life people disappoint you. They are cruel, and life is cruel. I think there is no win in life. Reality is a very painful, tough thing that you have to learn and cope with in some way. What we do is escape into fantasy, and it does give us moments of relief."

Some relief, perhaps but I would say mostly grief. The vanity of life is seen when we pursue human wisdom. One gives this insightful comment:

"One book in scripture that is expressly designed to turn us into realists is the book of Ecclesiastes…What the preacher wants to show us is that the real basis of wisdom is a frank acknowledgment that this world's course is [mysterious], that much of what happens is [unexplainable] to us, and that most occurrences "under the sun" bear no outward sign of a rational, moral God, ordering them all…Look says the preacher at the sort of world we live in…What do you see? Your life's background is set by aimlessly reoccurring cycles in nature. You see its shape fixed by times and circumstances over which you have no control; You see death coming to everyone sooner or later, but coming haphazardly — good men die like bad men; wise men like fools. You see evil running rampant…

and you realize that God's ordering of events is inscrutable, much as you want to make it out, you cannot do so… But once you conclude that there really is no rhyme or reason in things, what profit, value, gain, point, or purpose can you find [in it all?]. And if life is senseless, then it is valueless – what value is there in working, building, making money, and seeking to change things that will not be changed! Be realistic, says the preacher. Face the facts of life! Why must we feel so sure that we will be able to understand and explain why things happen?" [Knowing God by J. I. Packer, p. 93, 94, 95]

Even when we include God in our thinking – we still cannot always make sense of life! I know we have a generation of so-called preachers out there who claim to have a hot line directly to God. A sort of grab it from God and blab it! But sooner or later we all end up with egg on our face and see our foolish pride pin us to the mat. And frankly that is good because it reminds us of the infinite gulf between God and man. He knows it all and we are those who every now and then seem to get hit in the head or something and think we are in that same category. We are not! Real wisdom is to rest in God whether we can figure Him out or not.

Missionary Gracia Burnham, who was held captive by terrorists in the Philippines for more than a year and whose husband was killed during the rescue, writes: "Sometimes I wonder, *Why did Martin die when everyone was praying he wouldn't? Why does Scripture lead you to believe that if you pray a certain way, you'll get what you pray for?* People all over the world were praying that we'd both get out alive, but we didn't." Her questions made her realize it isn't always easy to comprehend God's nature:

"I used to have this concept of what God is like, and how life's supposed to be because of that. But in the jungle, I learned I don't know as much about God as I thought I did. I don't have him in a theological box anymore. What I do know is that God is God—and I'm not. The world's in a mess because of sin, not God. Some awful things may happen to me, but God does what is right. And He makes good out of bad situations." [Corrie Cutrer, "Soul Survivor," Today's Christian Woman (July/Aug 2003), p. 50]

CHAPTER 5

Wolf Call

§

(The Way of Pleasure)

Flip, flop with kay-eye —
What a cutie pie I see
Oops shoopa doo-wah
Lips of honey that's for me

Shim sham shimmie
I might forget you baby, there's no doubt
I saw you standing 'gainst the wall
I whistled and I gave my all
Now don't tell me you don't fall
For that wolf call

Just a little kiss'll put me in a whirl
I'll never whistle dearie at another girl
You love me well we'll have a ball
Why do you try to stall
Now don't tell me you don't fall
For that wolf call
For that wolf call
For that wolf call
[From the movie Girl Happy]

LIFE THESE DAYS IS SATURATED with those who have the wolf call down to a science. But for both, those who call and those who fall, life is empty and unsatisfying. If sexual saturation brought satisfaction we would be the most exciting generation that ever lived – but we are certainly not.

Billy Graham noted:

"America is said to have the highest per capita boredom of any spot on earth! We know that because we have the greatest number of artificial amusements of any country. People have become so empty that they can't even entertain themselves. They have to pay other people to amuse them, to make them laugh, to try to make them feel warm and happy and comfortable for a few minutes, to try to lose that awful, frightening, hollow feeling; that terrible, dreaded feeling of being lost and alone." [Billy Graham, as quoted by George Sweeting in Great Quotes and Illustrations, (Word, 1985)].

We are a nation in pursuit of pleasure – but our pleasure loving people are empty as ever!

Teacher: [1] I said to myself, "Let me dabble and test you in pleasure and see if there is any good in that." But look, that, too, was fleeting. [2] Of laughter I said, "Foolishness." Of pleasure, "And in the end what is accomplished?"

[3] So I thought about drinking wine, for it soothes the flesh. But all the while my mind was filled with thoughts of wisdom— about how to rein in foolishness— until I might understand the best way for us to live out our brief lives and number of days under heaven. [4] Next, I began some enormous projects, building my own houses and planting my own vineyards. [5] I designed impressive gardens and parks and planted them with all kinds of fruit trees. [6] I installed pools of water to irrigate the forests of young saplings. [7] I acquired male and female servants; I even had servants born into my household. I had herds of cattle, flocks of sheep and goats— more than anyone who had ever lived in Jerusalem before me. [8] I amassed a fortune in silver and gold, and I stockpiled the treasures of kings and provinces. I hired men and women to sing and entertain me, and I pampered myself with what every man desires— many women. [9] I surrounded myself with all this and became great, far greater than anyone who had ever lived in Jerusalem before

me. And still, my wisdom never left my side. [10]Throughout this experiment, I let myself have anything my eyes desired, and I did not withhold from my mind any pleasure. What was the conclusion? My mind found joy in all the work I did— my work was its own reward! [11]As I continued musing over all I had accomplished and the hard work it took, I concluded that all this, too, was fleeting, like trying to embrace the wind. Is there any real gain by all our hard work under the sun?

[Nelson, Thomas (2012-04-10). The Voice Bible: Step Into the Story of Scripture (pp. 771-772). Thomas Nelson. Kindle Edition]

THE TEST

I said in my heart, "Come now, I will test you – Ogden, "The important verb in this verse is the verb test. As soon as we see it, we know that the preacher is *not* just seeking pleasure for the sake of a good time. He was very scientific and wanted to know honestly whether pleasure could help him find "lasting benefits."

THE TESTED

with mirth; therefore enjoy pleasure – the root word of "mirth" is that of being glad or rejoicing." Pleasure refers to foolish pleasure, self-indulgent, frivolous merrymaking. Sort of reminded me of Ernest Hemingway, born in 1899, his whole life seemed to be designed to test the value of pleasure. At age 25 he sipped champagne in Paris, and later had well-publicized game hunts in Africa and hunted grizzly bears in America's northwest. At the age of sixty-one, after having it all wine, women, song, a distinguished literary career, Sunday afternoon bullfights in Spain. Finally Hemingway chose to end his life, leaving a note saying, "Life is one [expletive] thing after another." [Gary D. Preston, "Our Endless Pursuit of Pleasure," Discipleship Journal (Nov/Dec 1983)]

THE TRUTH HE FOUND

but surely, this also was vanity – he lets us know, up front, that pleasure could not provide the satisfaction he was longing for. Reminds me, of that Peggy Lee's hit song, called, "Is that all there is."

"Is that all there is? Is that all there is, my friend.

If that's all there is, we'll keep on dancing,

Let's break out the booze, and have a ball.

If that's all there is."

[Wikipedia.org., is that all there is]

The problem is if you break out all of the booze on the planet and seek to have a mega ball, you would still ultimately remain feeling as vacant and abandoned as ever! One noted, "Solomon pursued pleasure as a lab rat. He stimulated himself with wine…and took notes. What did he find? Why does pursuing pleasure ultimately end in futility? Because no matter how much fun you have, at some point you have to wake up to the real world. Pleasure will make you mad or crazy because you have to deny the reality that life is filled with pain. A life based on pleasure doesn't have room for getting fired from a job, seeing a loved one waste away with cancer, or having a child die in a car accident. The only way to live for pleasure is to deny reality…but reality refuses to be forever denied!"

THE TIRESOME SEARCH

PLEASURE IN *LAUGHTER*

I said of laughter--"Madness!"; and of mirth, "What does it accomplish?" – what possible lasting benefit could one derive from mere laughter? In Solomon's day they had those court Jesters, people who got by in life by making people laugh. He was a clown with the mission of making the one with the crown and his associate's chuckle with amusement.

In our day we have a glut of highly paid comedians whose job it is to keep us laughing – Jim Carey; Steve Martin; Richard Prior; Steve Harvey, etc. We love to laugh with the sitcoms – even reruns of *I Love Lucy; Andy Griffith; etc.;* they still put an occasional smile on our faces. Sadly the new sitcoms are not so pure in their antics. Barbra Bush said, "Everything is amusing these days: adultery; drunkenness; rebellious children; homosexuals. All are presented with quips and double-takes, and giggles. We find ourselves snickering at the very things God condemns." Billy Graham tells about a patient who consulted with a psychiatrist for help. He suffered from deep depression. Nothing he tried helped him. The psychiatrist told him about an Italian clown that was in town. He recommended that he go and hear him, saying a good night of laughter would do him good. With a look of despair on his face the man blurted out, "I am that clown!"

Pleasure in getting *Loaded* or *Lit up*

[3] *I searched in my heart how to gratify [stimulate] my flesh with wine, while guiding my heart with wisdom, and how to lay hold on [embracing] folly, till I might see what was good for the sons of men to do under heaven all the days of their lives* — obviously Solomon got drunk! Some say that he was just a connoisseur of wine, merely tasting it but the language seems to go beyond just a wine taster! The phrase, "and how to lay hold on folly demonstrates how far the preacher went in his testing for the pleasure wine could bring. He got drunk. The conjunction *"and"* does not add new action but shows how far he went in doing what he did." [A Hand book on Ecclesiastes by Ogden and Zogbo, p. 54].

Of course drunkenness is condemned in the Bible by none other than Solomon himself: Prov. 20:1; 23:20-21; 29-35.

Dean Martin had a hit song called, *Little old wine drinking me*. I guess a preacher shouldn't know all of these songs but I wasn't born saved!

I'M PRAYING FOR A RAIN IN CALIFORNIA
SO THE GRAPES CAN GROW AND THEY CAN MAKE MORE WINE
AND I'M SITTING IN A HONKY TONK IN CHICAGO

WITH A BROKEN HEART AND A WOMAN ON MY MIND
I'LL ASK THE MAN, BEHIND THE BAR, FOR THE JUKEBOX
AND THE MUSIC TAKES ME BACK TO TENNESSEE
AND WHEN THEY ASK WHO'S THE FOOL IN THE CORNER, CRYING
I'LL SAY, LITTLE OLD WINE DRINKING ME

Only a fool gives himself to wine or any other alcoholic beverage. I read about a Delaware man who was preparing for a cookout and decided to use gunpowder instead of charcoal or lighter fluid to get the coals glowing in his grill. The result was it blew up on him, and he suffered burns on his hands and face. Police said the man had been drinking. There is a famous oil painting by Bosch called the "ship of fools." It now hangs in the Louvre in Paris the painting shows ten people aboard a small vessel, with two of them are overboard swimming around. The ship has no captain; everyone on the ship is too engaged in drinking, feasting, and singing to know where the ship is going. They are like those enjoying all the carnal pleasures of this world without knowing where they will end up after the party is over. Atop the mast hangs a bunch of dangling carrots and a man is climbing up to reach them. Above the carrots there is a human skull. That skull is the 13th head in the painting, symbolizing being unlucky. The idea is that these 12 fools, who think all is perfect, are sailing right to their demise.

PLEASURE THROUGH *LABOR*

ARCHITECTURE

[4] *I undertook great projects: I built houses for myself* — we build things but soon become disinterested in them. According to a survey by the American Institute of Architects, 64 percent of architecture firms are reporting increased interest in outdoor living spaces. People claim they want to built "a luxurious outdoor world" right in their backyard so they can escape their everyday lives, hang out as a family, and spend time outside while staying at home. But the evidence shows that most families don't actually spend time in their backyard retreats. A 2012 book titled *Life at Home in the Twenty-first Century* revealed the results of an in-depth study of middle-class Los Angeles families. Researchers from UCLA recorded hours of footage while carefully documenting how families actually spent their time. According to their research, children averaged fewer than 40 minutes per week in their yards. Adults logged less than 15 minutes per week. All of these families benefitted from sunny Southern California weather. They had built a lot of nice things but they just didn't use them. And they found a disconnect between reality and these peoples beliefs: They found most families told the researchers that they were using their backyards often, but the researchers' observations

proved otherwise. One of the researchers noted, "Rather than use their outdoor retreats, people would retreat by turning on a [TV, computer, or video game] screen. People don't like this image of their lives. So they don't acknowledge it."

[Matt Woodley, managing editor, PreachingToday.com; source: Laura Vanderkam, "Column: Backyards are highly overrated," USATODAY (10-4-12)]

HORTICULTURE

...and planted vineyards. [5] I made gardens and parks and planted all kinds of fruit trees in them. [6] I made reservoirs to water groves of flourishing trees. [7] I bought male and female slaves and had other slaves who were born in my house – again America is into gardens but they do not want to take the time to be gardeners! In *First Things First*, A. Roger Merrill tells of a business consultant who decided to landscape his grounds. He hired a woman with a doctorate in horticulture who was extremely knowledgeable. Because the business consultant was very busy and traveled a lot, he kept emphasizing to her the need to create his garden in a way that would require little or no maintenance on his part. He insisted on automatic sprinklers and other labor-saving devices. Finally she stopped and said, "There's one thing you need to deal with before we go any further. If there's no gardener, there's no garden!"

I would love to have a garden – but busting up the soil and fertilizing it and planting things – take too much time and effort!

AGRICULTURE

I also owned more herds and flocks than anyone in Jerusalem before me – I am always telling Ann we need a few cows! Maybe a horse or several goats...Trouble is livestock has to be feed and cared for and when all is said and done not as much fun as we think. Somebody gave me a goat once, after about a week he was so much trouble I gave him to my neighbor!

AMASSING WEALTH CULTURE

I amassed silver and gold for myself, and the treasure of kings and provinces – you cannot turn on the television without hearing a commercial for amassing silver and gold! "Hi! I'm William Devane!" A 2012 *Boston Globe* article asked the following question: Does money change you? The article, "Here in the home of the American dream, most people are convinced that gaining a lot of money ... wouldn't change who they are as people." But is that true? The article reported:

"As a mounting body of research is showing, wealth can actually change how we think and behave—and not for the better. Rich people have a harder time connecting with others, showing less empathy to the extent of dehumanizing those who are different from them. They are less charitable and generous. They are less likely to help someone in trouble. And they are more likely to defend an unfair status quo. If you think you'd behave differently in their place, meanwhile, you're probably wrong: These aren't just inherited traits, but developed ones. Money, in other words, changes who you are." [Britt Petterson, "Why it matters that our politicians are rich," Boston Globe (2-19-12)]

We say "Hey I am not wealthy! I am barely making a living. I say take a trip to Nicaragua and you will realize just how much stuff we have amassed! To help Americans understand poverty in its truest sense, Robert L. Heilbroner, a prominent U.S. economist, itemized the luxuries most U.S. citizens would have to abandon if they were to adopt the lifestyle of their 1.2 billion neighbors who truly live in poverty:

"We begin by invading the house of our American family to strip it of its furniture. Everything goes: beds, chairs, tables, television set, lamps. We will leave the family with a few old blankets, a kitchen table, a wooden chair. In relationship to clothes. Each member of the family may keep his oldest suit or dress, a shirt or blouse. We will permit a pair of shoes for the head of the family, but none for the wife or children. We move to the kitchen. The appliances have already been taken out, so we turn to the cupboards. ...The box of matches may stay, a small bag of flour, some sugar, and salt. A few moldy potatoes, already in the garbage can, must be hastily rescued, for they will provide much of tonight's meal. We will leave a handful of onions, and a dish of dried beans. All the rest we take away: the meat, the fresh vegetables, the canned goods, the crackers, the candy. Now we [strip] the [rest of the] house: the bathroom...[is] dismantled, the running water shut off, the electric wires taken out. Next we take away the house. The family can move to the tool shed....Communications must go next. No more newspapers, magazines, books—not that they are missed, since we must take away our

family's literacy as well. Instead, in our shantytown we will allow one radio…
Now government services must go. No more postman, no more firemen. There
is a school, but it is three miles away and consists of two classrooms…There
are, of course, no hospitals or doctors nearby. The nearest clinic is ten miles
away and is tended by a midwife. It can be reached by bicycle, provided that the
family has a bicycle, which is unlikely…Finally, money. We will allow our family…$5." [Robert L. Heilbroner, The Great Ascent: The Struggle for Economic
Development in Our Time (New York: Harper & Row, 1963), pp. 33-36]

Let's face it – we are all by comparison wealthy! We have far more wealth
than Solomon ever dreamed of, and yet like him we find no fulfillment in the
things we have.

ARRAY OF MUSIC CULTURE

…I acquired male and female singers… - this is a generation that seeks to find
meaning in music! We have our Pandora; our iPods; our iTunes; our Spotify;
and the beat goes on…and on! According to a recent study by the Kaiser Family
Foundation, kids aged 8 to 18 years devote an average of 7 hours and 38 minutes per day to entertainment media. That's more than 53 hours a week. And
because they spend so much of that time doing what researchers call media mul-
titasking—for example, surfing the Internet while listening to music—they
actually manage to amass a total of 10 hours and 45 minutes worth of media
content in those 7 hours and 38 minutes. [Bill White, Paramount, California;
source: Leadership Network Advance on-line digest (3-9-10)]

The number one way we American's deal with stress is listening to
music. Studies show 52% say that's how we deal with stress. I suppose I get
more pleasure out of music then most things. If I cannot sleep at night I listen to music through my iPod; mowing the yard literally takes hours, but I
put on my head phones and dance to the music, it makes life bearable. And
yet, I get tired of music, it seems like after a while, it's all the same stuff.
So Solomon labored in Architecture; Horticulture; Agriculture; Amassing
culture; and an Array of music culture – but all his labors left him just as
empty as ever. Like Raquel Welch who said, "I thought it was very peculiar
that I had acquired everything I had wanted as a child – wealth, fame and

accomplishment in my career, I had beautiful children and a lifestyle that seemed terrific, and yet, I was totally and miserably unhappy. I found it very frightening, that one could acquire all these things, and still be so miserable." [SermonCentral.com, Raquel Welch Was One Of Hollywood's Most Famous]

PLEASURE THROUGH LUST

...and the pleasures of men—many concubines - Solomon was the Hugh Hefner of his day!

He had seven hundred wives, princesses, and three hundred concubines, and his wives turned his heart away. 1 Kings 11:3

America is a slave to lustful pleasures. Just Consider the following:

* Every 39 Minutes a porn movie is made;
* $380 dollars is spent per second on porn;
* The number of porn sites in 1998: 71,831
* In 2001: 311,652
* In 2003: 1.3 million

Ex-porn star Traci Lords, who got into the "adult entertainment" business as a 15-year-old said, "I can tell you from personal experience that I've never met a happy porn star." [Dateline NBC (7-11-03); found in Citizen magazine (October 2003), p. 15]

Lust always leaves one unfulfilled and empty...

THE TROUBLING SUMMATION

HE WAS RECOGNIZED

[9] *So I became great and excelled more than all who were before me in Jerusalem. Also my wisdom remained with me* – how many think that if they could just be famous, well known, important, and looked up to they would be happy. Actor Jim Carry said, "I think everybody should get rich and famous and do everything they ever dreamed of so they can see that it's not the answer."

HE WAS NOT RESTRAINED

[10] *Whatever my eyes desired I did not keep from them. I did not withhold my heart from any pleasure, For my heart rejoiced in all my labor; And this was my reward from all my labor* – he sought out every conceivable pleasure! He was not alone:

* People seek pleasure in unbelief— Voltaire was an infidel of the most pronounced type. He wrote: "I wish I had never been born."
* People seek pleasure in pleasure – Lord Byron lived a life of pleasure, if anyone did. He wrote: "The worm, the canker, and the grief are mine alone."
* People seek pleasure in money— Jay Gould, the American millionaire, had plenty of that.
  When dying he said: "I suppose I am the most miserable man on earth."
* People seek pleasure in position and fame— Lord Beaconsfield enjoyed more than his share of both. He wrote: "Youth is a mistake; manhood, a struggle; old age, regret."
* People seek pleasure in military glory— Alexander the Great conquered the known world in his day. Having done so, he wept, because, he said, "There are no more worlds to conquer."

HE TEMPORARILY REJOICED

...For my heart rejoiced in all my labor; And this was my reward from all my labor – yes, he had brief moments of joy in all his labors. But it just doesn't last! F. W. Woolworth, founder of the Woolworth's chain of stores, had made one of the largest fortunes in the world by the early 1900s. A portion of this fortune, more than $50 million, was given to his granddaughter, Barbara Hutton, when she turned twenty-one in 1933.

Although she was one of the richest women in America, Barbara was never able to find personal happiness. She married 7 times (including among her husband's a prince; a count; and the actor Cary Grant). Hutton spent her life battling drug and alcohol dependency and anorexia, and her numerous divorces left her almost bankrupt. When the reclusive Hutton finally died at age sixty-six, she weighed less than one hundred pounds and only $3,000 of her fortune remained. I'm sure she experienced many moments of happiness during her life – but hours of emptiness! [A Life Well Lived, A Study of the Book of Ecclesiastes by Tommy Nelson, A King's Quest for Meaning, p. 28]

HE REFLECTED

Then I looked on all the works that my hands had done And on the labor in which I had toiled; And indeed all was vanity and grasping for the wind. There was no profit under the sun – he gave himself wholeheartedly to pleasure, but pleasure refused to return the favor! Perhaps you have seen the movie, *Out of Africa*. The movie is a nostalgic reflection of a young Danish woman named Karen Blixen. At an early age she goes to Kenya.

There she marries a man she hardly knows; she plants a coffee plantation; and for a while, paradise belongs to Karen. Then, after about 15 years of hard labor, within the span of a few months she loses it all. She loses her health, she loses her lover, she loses her friends, she loses her coffee crop and her farm, and finally she loses her identity. Everything she lived for has been taken away from her. As she is reflecting—she writes about how meaningless it all was. She says:

"If I know a song for Africa, of the giraffe and the African new moon lying on her back, of the plows in the fields and the sweaty faces of the coffee pickers, does Africa know a song of me? Would the air over the plain quiver with a color that I had had on? Or the children invent a game in which my name was? Or the full moon throw a shadow over the gravel of the drive that was like me? Or would the eagles of the hills look out for me?"

She had given her life to Africa, but when she's gone, Africa doesn't remember her. There's nothing there that remembers her, though she remembers it.

Pleasure is like that – you may give you life to it; but it will not giving anything of value back to you. Vanity in life is seen in the Way of Pleasure. Let's be clear, God is the creator of pleasure, as C. S Lewis noted in Screwtape:

"Never forget, that when we are dealing with any pleasure, in its healthy and normal and satisfying form, we are on the Enemies [God's] ground. I know we have won many a soul through pleasure. All the same, it is His invention, not ours. He makes pleasure; all of our research so far, has not enabled us, to produce one. All we can do, is to encourage the humans, to take the pleasures which our Enemy has produced, and use them in ways which He has forbidden."

[C. S. Lewis, The Screwtape Letters and Screwtape Proposes a Toast (London: Geoffrey Bles, 1960), p. 50]

The problem comes when we abuse pleasure by building our lives upon it – it is always a byproduct not the pursuit of our lives.

James Dobson said it well, "I feel the need to stress, what I consider to be the fundamental cause, of a mid-life crisis. It results, from what the Bible refers to as, building your house upon the sand. It is possible, to be a follower of Jesus Christ and accept His forgiveness from sin, yet still be deeply influenced by the values and attitudes, of one's surrounding culture. Thus a young Christian husband and father may become a workaholic; a hoarder of money; a status-seeker; a worshipper of youth; a *lover of pleasure*. These tendencies may not reflect his conscious choices and desires; they merely represent the stamp of society's godless values, on his life and times. Despite his unchristian attitudes, the man may appear, to have it all together in his first 15 years as an adult, especially if he is successful in early business pursuits. But he is in considerable danger. Whenever we build our lives on values and principles that contradict, the time-honored wisdom of God's Word, we are laying a foundation on the sand. Sooner or later, the storms will howl, and the structure, we have laboriously constructed will collapse with a mighty crash."

CHAPTER 6

We're Gonna Move

§

(We all Wind up dead)

Well there's a leak in this old building
Yes, there's a leak in this old building
Well there's a leak in this old building
We're gonna move to a better home
We got no pane in this old window'
We got no pane in this old window'
We got no pane in this old window'
We're gonna move to a better home
Well there's a hole in the roof where the rain pours in; A hole in the floor where
it drops right out again
Well there's a leak in this old building
Well there's a leak in this old building
Well there's a leak in this old building
We're gonna move to a better home
Well there's a crack across the ceiling
Yes there's a crack across the ceiling
Well there's a crack across the ceiling
We're gonna find us a better home
We've gotta stove without a chimney
We've gotta stove without a chimney
What good's a stove without a chimney
We're gonna move to a better home.
[From the Album *A Date with Elvis*]

OUR BODIES ARE COMPARED TO a house, and the older we get the more it seems to be falling apart! But the good news for the believer is that we are gonna move to a new, glorified one. But since we are in a context of living under the sun – not so fast! That move, what the world knows as death, is not something those locked into this world like to think about. In an 2012 interview with the actor and film director Woody Allen the article noted that "Allen has been confronting the horror of mortality … since he was five." Allen said:

> "There's no advantage to aging. You don't get wiser, you don't get more mellow, you don't see life in a more glowing way. You have to fight your body decaying, and you have less options. The only thing you can do is what you did when you were 20—because you're always walking with an abyss right under your feet … which is to distract yourself. Getting involved in a movie [occupies] all my anxiety … If I wasn't concentrated on [distractions], I'd be thinking of larger issues. And those aren't resolvable, and you're checkmated whichever way you go."

[Oliver Burkeman, "Woody Allen: 'To have been a lead character in a juicy scandal doesn't bother me,'" The Guardian, (9-13-12)]

Woody Allen is obviously lost and is a good illustration of what life is like if you leave God and eternity out of the picture. He would be a good one to pray for before his appointment with death is upon him. Truth is, there is always a possibility that Death's Door will swing wide open at any moment – we never know when it's going to grab a hold of us and pull us in! The vanity of life is seen in the fact that we all Wind up dead. Notice the focus is on death - 2:12-26, vv. 12b, 14b, 15, 16b, 18, 21, 26.

[12]I turned my attention to the ways of wisdom and folly and madness. I asked, "What is left for those who come after the king to do? They can only repeat what he has already done."* [13]I realized that wisdom is better than folly, just as light is better than darkness. [14]As the old saying goes: The wise have eyes in their heads, but fools stumble in the darkness. Yet I knew deep down that the same fate comes to both of them. [15]I said to myself, "Why do I try to be wise when my fate is the same as that of the fool? This pursuit is fleeting too." [16]Neither the wise nor the fool

will be remembered for very long once they are gone. The wise dies, and the fool alike. All are forgotten in the future. [17]So I began to hate life itself because all that is done under the sun is so harsh and difficult. Life— everything about it— is fleeting; it's like trying to pursue the wind. [18]So I began to hate all the hard work I had done under the sun because I would eventually have to leave it all to the one who comes after me. [19]And who knows whether my heir will be wise or foolish? Still he will inherit all the things for which I worked so hard here under the sun, the things for which I became wise. This, too, is fleeting like trying to catch hold of a breath. [20]So I turned these thoughts over in my mind and despaired over how hard I worked under the sun. [21]Although someone with wisdom, knowledge, and skill works hard, when he departs this life, he will leave all he has accomplished to another who has done nothing to deserve work's reward. This, too, is fleeting, and it causes great misery. [22]What exactly do people get out of all their work and all the stresses they put themselves through here under the sun? [23]For every day is filled with pain and every job has its own problems, and there are nights when the mind doesn't stop and rest. And once again, this is fleeting. [24]There is nothing better than for people to eat and drink and to see the good in their hard work. These beautiful gifts, I realized, too, come from God's hand. [25]For who can eat and drink and enjoy the good things if not me? [26]To those who seek to please God, He gives wisdom and knowledge and joyfulness; but to those who are wicked, God keeps them busy harvesting and storing up for those in whom He delights. But even this is fleeting; it's like trying to embrace the wind. [Nelson, Thomas (2012-04-10). The Voice Bible: Step Into the Story of Scripture (p. 772). Thomas Nelson. Kindle Edition]

AT DEATH WE ARE *FOLLOWED* BY SOMEBODY WHO CAN DO NO MORE THEN WE DID

Then I turned myself to consider wisdom and madness and folly; For what can the man do who succeeds the king?-- Only what he has already done - the king suggests that it is folly for successive generations to make the same experiments, seeking to find the meaning to life, when they can learn from Solomon that life, under the sun, is meaningless and there is nothing new – at best they can only waste their time repeating what he has already done.

The city of Ann Arbor, Michigan, is home to one of the most fascinating museums on the planet. The facility goes under the name of the "Museum of Failed Products." At first sight, the shelves and aisles look just like a supermarket —except there's only one of each item. And you won't find these items in a real supermarket they are failures, products withdrawn from sale after a few weeks or months, because almost nobody wanted to buy them. This is consumer capitalism's graveyard. It's the only place on the planet where you'll find: Clairol's A Touch of Yogurt shampoo alongside Gillette's equally unpopular For Oily Hair Only, a few feet from a now-empty bottle of Pepsi AM Breakfast Cola (born 1989; died 1990). The museum is home to discontinued brands of caffeinated beer; to Fortune Snookies, a short-lived line of fortune cookies for dogs; to self-heating soup cans that had a tendency to explode in customers' faces; and to packets of breath mints that had to be withdrawn from sale because they looked like tiny packages of crack cocaine.

The book of Ecclesiastes is the Museum of Failed Pursuits – he is warning us not to pursue things that give no purpose or meaning to life as he did. He wants us to learn from his mistakes but he knows that often we will not...

DEATH MUST BE *FACED* BY BOTH THE WISE AND THE FOOLISH

[13] *Then I saw that wisdom excels folly As light excels darkness.* [14] *The wise man's eyes are in his head, But the fool walks in darkness. Yet I myself perceived That the same event happens to them all* – it doesn't matter whether you're the head of the Central Intelligent agency or a bus driver in Decatur! Both the intelligent and the idiot die! The truth is we all die! No one is too old to die and no one is too young.

Often called, the shortest and most complete story in English, supposedly written by Ernest Hemingway, it is only six words long: "For sale: baby shoes, never worn." Death comes to the Strong as well as the weak.

In April, 2011, *Newsweek* magazine featured an article about Arnold Schwarzenegger, movie star and former governor of California. Here are some of the most telling excerpts from the article: At 63, Arnold Schwarzenegger said, "I feel terrific about where I am in my life, when I look back at what I've accomplished, but I feel [horrible] when I look at myself in the mirror." Schwarzenegger—a five-time Mr. Universe and seven-time Mr. Olympia now the 31-inch waist has ballooned to 36, and the vaunted 57-inch chest has shrunk by a half foot. He said, "When I stand in front of a mirror and really look, I wonder: What the [heck] happened here?" Thirteen years ago, when he was 50, Schwarzenegger had surgery to replace a defective aortic valve ...At some point in the next several years the valve will wear out, and surgeons will split his chest open to install a new one. He said, "It does quite a number on you for quite some time, because even though you're strong willed, you know from now on your damaged goods. As with most things, I live in denial." His mentor and good friend Joe Weider died just the other week, another reminder that in spite of our strength we all must die just like the weakling!

In his book *Spirit Life*, D. Stuart Briscoe writes, "When I moved to the United States, I was impressed with the number of total strangers who visited my home to wish me well—they all sold insurance! One day my visitor was talking about the necessity to be prudent in the preparation for all possibilities. "If something should happen to you, Mr. Briscoe..." he started to say, but I interrupted with, "please don't say that. It upsets me." He was a little startled, but tried again, 'But with all due respects, sir, we must be ready if something should happen to us.' 'Don't say that,' I insisted. he looked totally bewildered and said, 'I don't understand what I said to upset you.' 'Then I'll tell you,' I replied. 'It upsets me that you talk about (life's) only certainty as if it's a possibility. Death isn't a possibility, it's a certainty. You don't say "If," you say "When," whenever death is the subject.'"

AFTER DEATH ALL WILL BE *FORGOTTEN*

[15] *So I said in my heart, "As it happens to the fool, It also happens to me, And why was I then more wise?" Then I said in my heart, "This also is vanity."* [16] *For there is no more remembrance of the wise than of the fool forever, Since all that now is will be forgotten in the days to come. And how does a wise man die? As the fool!* – we will all eventually be forgotten. Yes, even people like Elvis Presley as hard as that might be for some to accept. *Citizen Kane*, directed by Orson Welles, traces the life of fictional

newspaper tycoon Charles Foster Kane from childhood to his deathbed. The film pieces together witnesses' testimonies of Kane's tumultuous personality and lifestyle, as news reporter Jerry Thompson tries to determine the meaning of Kane's dying word: *Rosebud*. Throughout the film, Thompson learns that Kane looked for love and fulfillment in many ways. Kane rescued a dying newspaper. He married for love and then left his first wife to pursue a relationship and marriage with his mistress. He even constructed an elaborate palace (Xanadu) and filled it with riches from around the world. But Kane died alone and forgotten. And when he died, he thought only of *Rosebud*. As the film comes to a close, Thompson walks around the basement of the palace, staring at all of Kane's wealth. He says, "I guess *Rosebud* is just a piece in a jigsaw puzzle a missing piece." While workers shovel trash into a furnace, the camera rests on a pile of burning junk. Kane's abandoned wooden sled burns on the top of the pile. Amidst the flames, you can decipher one word on the sled: *Rosebud*. [Citizen Kane (RKO Pictures, 1941), rated PG, written by Orson Welles & Herman J. Mankiewicz, directed by Orson Welles; submitted by Mary Lasse, Aurora, Illinois]

Life is like that, we are not really remembered, everything we have eventually gets burned up, and we become just a missing piece of a jigsaw puzzle that doesn't make sense. One of my favorite preachers is Charles Haddon Spurgeon; He was born in England in 1834. He became a Christian and preached his first sermon at the age of sixteen. At the age of nineteen he preached as a guest in the famous but mostly lifeless New Park Street Chapel in London. Only two hundred people came to the 1200-seat sanctuary. By the age of twenty-one, he had taken over the full-time pastorate of this historic congregation. Within a year, New Park Street Chapel had to be enlarged to seat the crowds who came to hear him preach. Yet still more people came to hear him preach, so in 1861 the church moved into the Metropolitan Tabernacle which could accommodate sixty-five hundred people.

His sermons were so popular that a publisher printed and sold one sermon each week for more than twenty-seven years. This preacher not only started orphanages to care for thousands of children but he also influenced the lives of businessman, government officials, and kings. When he died in 1892, Spurgeon was perhaps the most famous man in the world. One man who recently went to London to see Spurgeons great church, ask several people to direct him to Spurgeons church and they all said, "Spurgeon who?" My email is supurgeonwannabe@yahoo.com. I have shared it with many people and most of them ask, "What is a spurgeon?"

What He *Found* About Death Caused Him To Despair

DISSATISFACTION

[17] *Therefore I hated life because the work that was done under the sun was distressing to me, for all is vanity and grasping for the wind* - Reminds me of something I read the other day:

Are You Tired? The population of this country is 220 million; 84 million are over 60 years of age, which leaves 136 million to do the work.

People under 20 years of age total 95 million, which leaves 41 million to do the work. There are 22 million who are employed by the government, which leaves 19 million to do the work. Four million are in the armed forces, which leave 15 million to do the work. Deduct 14,800,000—the number in state and city offices, leaving 200,000 to do the work. There are 188,000 in hospitals, insane asylums, etc.—that leaves 12,000 people to do the work. Now it may interest you to know that there are 11,998 people in jail, so that leaves just two people to carry the load and that's you and me, brother, and I'm getting tired of doing everything myself!

DEATH

[18] *Then I hated all my labor in which I had toiled under the sun, because I must leave it to the man who will come after me.* [19] *And who knows whether he will be wise or a fool? Yet he will rule over all my labor in which I toiled and in which I have shown myself wise under the sun. This also is vanity* — as Billy Graham said, when asked if he know how much Howard Hughes left behind. He said, "Yes, I know exactly how much he left behind — he left it all!"

DISCONTENTMENT

[20] *Therefore I turned my heart and despaired of all the labor in which I had toiled under the sun.* [21] *For there is a man whose labor is with wisdom, knowledge, and skill; yet he must*

leave his heritage to a man who has not labored for it. This also is vanity and a great evil. *[22] For what has man for all his labor, and for the striving of his heart with which he has toiled under the sun? [23] For all his days are sorrowful, and his work burdensome; even in the night his heart takes no rest. This also is vanity* - He felt like Woody Allen who said, "<u>Life is divided into the horrible and the miserable.</u>" Albert Camus wrote, *The Fall*, which tells of a Persian Lawyer sitting by a river bank, thinking over his life. His mind goes back to a day when he was rushing to get to Court on time. He crosses over a bridge and hears a woman crying out for help – she was in the water drowning. He stops and watches but realizes that if he helps her he will be late for his court appointment. So he continues on his way as the screams get dimmer and dimmer. Now years later he sits by another river bank. He can again hear that woman's screaming out for help. He says:

> "Oh young woman, throw yourself again into that river!" The implica-
> tion is if only he had another chance things would be different. Then he
> says, "Awe, but it's too late…it's always too late."

When Solomon comes to the end of his life, he looks back and feels the sting of regret. Things rarely go as we would like them to. By the way Albert Camus once said that he couldn't imagine a death more meaningless than dying in a car accident. In 1960, at the age of 47, Camus died in a car accident!

DEATH CAN BE ENDURED ONLY WHEN GOD IS *FACTORED* IN
THE ONLY SATISFIER

[24] Nothing is better for a man than that he should eat and drink, and that his soul should enjoy good in his labor. This also, I saw, was from the hand of God. [25] For who can eat, or who can have enjoyment, more than I? - He comes up for a gulp of air! If we add God into the equation everything we do takes on significance and joy. In 2002, Marvin Lacy of Lake Wales Florida taught calligraphy in the local area. What makes that special is the great-grandfather of five suffers from Parkinson's disease. The disease often makes his hands tremble. Though he has this disease, when Marvin sits down to create his works of calligraphy, his hands are suddenly stable and become still. Marvin says, "It's a gift from God." Lacy's

faith influences all that he does. He says, "The Lord is important in my life. I wouldn't want to leave out that aspect of my life. One of the sayings I've put into calligraphy is a philosophy I picked up.

'I will make that which I do today important. I am exchanging a day of my life for it.'"

Lacy's specialty is calligraphic works of art, including wall hangings and greeting cards. His work ranges from Bible passages to the comical sayings. He adds, "The scripture says that a merry heart does good like medicine. To me, that kind of stuff is fun." [Fresh Illustrations, Contentment By Jim Wilson]

THE SOURCE

26 For God gives wisdom and knowledge and joy to a man who is good in His sight; but to the sinner He gives the work of gathering and collecting, that he may give to him who is good before God. This also is vanity and grasping for the wind- notice the repetition of "God gives...He gives..." The God above the sun is the source of our life under the sun! Reminded me of two brothers, Geze and Zslot Peladi, who were literally living in a cave near Budapest for years. They left their dark, sunless home by selling scrap metal and candy. Theirs was a hopeless situation.

But then everything changed. One day, out of the blue, charity workers informed the brothers that they had inherited a substantial portion of their late maternal grandmother's $6.6 billion fortune. And just like that, two destitute brothers, should they want to, could call a castle their home when all they had ever known was a cave. [Brian Lowery, managing editor, PreachingToday.com]

Living under the sun is cave living; but when we focus on Jesus Christ we find we are joint heirs with Him and seated in the heavenlies in Christ! If we include God and eternity, both life and death take on a whole new perspective. In the 1960s, there was an American girl attending college in Switzerland. At the school she met a lot of young postmodern Europeans. They were steeped in philosophy, humanism, atheism, and nihilism, and some of them doubted that they even existed. They had no reference point—other than their own emotions and insight—to make sense of the world. But his American girl said,

"Because I believe that the infinite, personal God made us, and we're not simply part of nature. We are created in the image of God. Evil is not just something out there that looks unpleasant; it is truly evil because it's contrary to Him. God has made Himself known in the Bible. The paramount idea of the Bible is the person of Jesus Christ who came to save us from sin. Through Him we can know God and enjoy everything He has given. We can die in hope." They asked her how she learned such things? She told them she had learned them from her father. She eventually brought them to meet her father, Francis Schaeffer, who show them how their worldview ultimately ended in despair. The result was more then a few of these young people trusted Christ, and soon people from all over the world were coming to *L'Abri,"* the shelter."

[A Life Well Lived, Solomon gives us the Answer, A Study of the Book of Ecclesiastes by Tommy Nelson p. 39].

The vanity of life is seen in the fact we all Wind up dead. Woody Allen said he began worrying about death when he was just 5 years old; today he is in his late 70s. (He was born Dec. 1, 1935). Here are some amusing quotes by Woody:

"I don't want to achieve immortality through my work...I want to achieve it through not dying." Woody Allen

"It is impossible to experience one's death objectively and still carry a tune." Woody Allen

"Life is full of misery, loneliness, and suffering - and it's all over much too soon." Woody Allen

CHAPTER 7

Where do you come from?

§

(Can't figure out the Ways of God)
Eccles. 3:1-4:3

Where do you come from?
Tell me who you are
Do you come from another world
Or from some distant star?

Where do you come from?
Are you what you seem?
Are you real,
Are you standing there,
Or is it just a dream?

Tell me more about yourself
Do you feel the way I feel?
Are you just a vision,
Or are you really real?

Where do you come from?
Angel won't you say?
Tell me all that there is to know
And tell me that you'll stay.
[From the Movie, Girls! Girls! Girls! 1962]

TEACHER: 1FOR EVERYTHING THAT HAPPENS in life— there is a season, a right time for everything under heaven: 2A time to be born, a time to die; a time to plant, a time to collect the harvest; 3A time to kill, a time to heal; a time to tear down, a time to build up; 4A time to cry, a time to laugh; a time to mourn, a time to dance; 5A time to scatter stones, a time to pile them up; a time for a warm embrace, a time for keeping your distance; 6A time to search, a time to give up as lost; a time to keep, a time to throw out; 7A time to tear apart, a time to bind together; a time to be quiet, a time to speak up; 8A time to love, a time to hate; a time to go to war, a time to make peace. 9What good comes to anyone who works so hard, all to gain a few possessions? 10I have seen the kinds of tasks God has given each of us to do to keep one busy, 11and I know God has made everything beautiful for its time. God has also placed in our minds a sense of eternity; we look back on the past and ponder over the future, yet we cannot understand the doings of God. 12I know there is nothing better for us than to be joyful and to do good throughout our lives; 13to eat and drink and see the good in all of our hard work is a gift from God. 14I know everything God does endures for all time. Nothing can be added to it; nothing can be taken away from it. We humans can only stand in awe of all God has done.

15What has been and what is to be— already is. And God holds accountable all the pursuits of humanity. Teacher: 16Again, I looked at everything that goes on under the sun and realized that in place of justice, wickedness prevails. In place of righteousness, wrongdoing succeeds. 17I said to myself, "God will judge the righteous and the wicked, for there is a right time for every pursuit and for every action."* 18I thought about how people act: "God often puts them to the test to show them how much they are like the animals." 19The fate of humans and the fate of animals is the same. As one dies, so does the other, for we have the same breath within us. In the end, we have no advantage over the animals. For as I have said, it's all fleeting. 20Humans and animals alike go to one place; all are formed from dust, and all return to the dust once more. 21Who really knows whether the spirits of human beings go up and the spirits of animals go down into the earth? 22So I realized there is nothing better for us than to find joy in the work we do, for work is its own reward. For who will bring us back to see what will be after we are gone?

Teacher: 1Then I looked again and saw all the oppression that happens under the sun. I saw the tears of the oppressed, and no one offered to help and comfort them. The oppressors exercise all the power, while the powerless have no one to help and comfort them. 2It struck me that the dead are actually better off than the living who must go on living; 3and, even better, are those who were never born in the first place. At least they have never had to witness all of the injustices that take place under the sun. [Nelson, Thomas (2012-04-10). The Voice Bible: Step Into the Story of Scripture (p. 772-773). Thomas Nelson. Kindle Edition]

Where do we come from? Why are we here? Where are we going? Why does this or that happen? We usually are left scratching our heads. We are not sure why things happen or where life smacking us in the head comes from but one thing we can probably all agree on is this is not the way we would do things!

Judith Viorst wrote, from the perspective of a 6 year old, "If I were in charge of the World and other Worries."

"If I were in charge of the world
I'd cancel oatmeal,
Monday mornings,
Allergy shots.

If I were in charge of the world
There'd be brighter night lights,
Healthier hamsters, and
Basketball baskets 48 inches lower.

If I were in charge of the world
You wouldn't have lonely,
You wouldn't have clean,
You wouldn't have bedtime,
Or, "Don't punch your sister."
In fact, you wouldn't even have sisters.

If I were in charge of the world
A chocolate sundae with whipped cream and nuts would be a vegetable.

All 007 movies would be rated G.
And a person who sometimes forgets to brush,
And sometimes forgets to flush,
Would be allowed to be
In charge of the world."
[http://poetryforchildren.tripod.com]

If we were in charge of this world things would be a lot different – there would be no need for dentist; cars would always start; there would be no finical problems; there would be no empty pew; nobody would ever get sick; and the grass would never need to be cut.

The world would be different but not better! God alone knows what is for our ultimate good and what is not. Vanity is seen in the fact that we cannot figure out the Ways of God.

God's Sovereign Ways In The *Seasons* Of Life
The Principle
To everything there is a season, A time for every purpose under heaven: - God is in control of the universe and has appointed a time for everything.

[20] Daniel answered and said: "Blessed be the name of God forever and ever, For wisdom and might are His. [21] And He changes the times and the seasons; He removes kings and raises up kings; He gives wisdom to the wise And knowledge to those who have understanding. [22] He reveals deep and secret things; He knows what *is* in the darkness, And light dwells with Him. Daniel 2:20-22

God has an eternal plan which cannot be anticipated as we live out our lives in time. As he looks back on his long life, Jayber Crow, the main character in Wendell Berry's novel, reflects on how God's guidance and providence often catch us by surprise. "I can't look back from where I am now and feel that I have been very much in charge of my life…I have made plans enough, but I see now that I have never lived by plan…Nearly everything that has happened to me has happened by surprise. All the important things have happened by surprise. And whatever has been happening usually has happened before I had time to expect it ….And so when I have thought I was in my story or in charge of it, I really have been only on the edge of it, carried along. Is this because we are in an eternal story that is happening [only] partly in time?" [Wendell Berry, Jayber Crow (Counterpoint, 2001), p. 322]

PURPOSES
We have both a Birthday and a Deathday
   A time to be born, And a time to die; A time to plant, And a time to pluck what is planted; – and we control neither! Notice even plants have a beginning and an end, and this planting and plucking is according to God's sovereign seasons.

God's purpose includes both things that are
Destructive and Constructive

A time to kill, And a time to heal; A time to break down, And a time to build up; – God's plan allows for both Murder and Medicine; Hurting and Healing; old buildings are constantly being torn down and new one's built.

There is a time for Gladness and Sadness

[4] *A time to weep, And a time to laugh; A time to mourn, And a time to dance;* - on some occasions we cry and on others we laugh; life consist of both funerals and weddings.

Time includes Removing and Receiving

[5] *A time to cast away stones, And a time to gather stones; A time to embrace, And a time to refrain from embracing;* - a time to remove stones, like when your clearing out a field; and a time to gather stones when you're about to build something. There is a time to hug, and a time when hugs, are not appropriate.

A time to Get and a time to Give

⁶A time to gain, And a time to lose; A time to keep, And a time to throw away; - sometimes you get things, at other times it off to helping hands.

A time for Mourning and a time for Mending

⁷A time to tear, And a time to sew; A time to keep silence, And a time to speak; - in Solomon's day grief was expressed by tearing one's garment (Gen. 37:29/2 Sam. 13:21). Afterwards those garments needed to be sowed back together. Sometimes silence is golden, at other times its yellow!

A time for Hostility and a time for Harmony

⁸A time to love, And a time to hate; A time of war, And a time of peace – not only to love but to hate! We should hate that which is evil (Rom.12:9). God's plan not only includes peace but also war. Peter Muhlenberg gave perhaps the most dramatic sermon of the Revolutionary era. Peter joined the army and decided that, in his last sermon before leaving, he would do something unusual to drive home his point. After reading from Ecclesiastes 3:1, he said, "There is a time to preach and a time to pray, but there is also a time to fight, and that time has now come." Peter threw off his robes to reveal the uniform of a militia colonel. He then recruited the men of his congregation, who became known as the "German Regiment," which Peter commanded throughout the war. He eventually rose to the rank of major general, and after the war, returned to Philadelphia a hero. He spent the remainder of his life in local and national politics. [Mark Couvillon. "The American Revolution," Christian History, no. 50.].

God's purposes cover a wide range of opposites. Life is a roller coaster ride! You never know what's coming at you – one day you have to duck the next day you have to pucker. We look at life and want to sing with Elvis, where do you come from! There was a tornado that came through Merritt Island, down in Florida. A lady, who lived in a trailer house, had a little parakeet. She loved that parakeet. The house trailer was devastated; the parakeet was gone. And, she missed the parakeet more than she missed the house trailer. Many days after the tornado, a person looked up in a tree, and there sat a parakeet; and, she was able to coax that bird out of that tree, set it on her finger. And, she began to inquire around, "Has anybody lost a parakeet?" And, they determined this lady had lost a parakeet. It seemed so miraculous. It was news in the newspaper: "The parakeet has been found after the tornado, sitting in a tree." They were trying to find something good about the disaster. But the very next day, a cat ate her parakeet! Who can figure it out?

The Chinese have a story about a man who had a prize horse, and the horse got loose and ran off. And, everybody said, "Oh, that's terrible." But, after a while, he came back, and he had some wild stallions with him. They said, "That's wonderful." But then, the man's son got on one of the wild stallions to break it in, and instead he broke his own leg. They said, "That's terrible." But then, there was a war, and the young man didn't have to go to war. And, they said, "That's good." Just when you think it's good, it's bad; just when you think it's bad, it's good. Like it or not life is that way, and we might as well accept it.

As Frank Sinatra used to sing, "That's Life!" That is truth, the whole truth, and nothing but the truth and it is a wise God who has engineered it that way.

The Problem

⁹ What profit has the worker from that in which he labors? ¹⁰ I have seen the God- given task with which the sons of men are to be occupied – Our problem is we do not want a life of ups and downs; or one of pain and pleasure; or good and evil – we want a life of all ups, all pleasure, all good.

Swindoll notes: "Solomon gave us a long list of opposites. Fourteen are positive and fourteen are negative. In some ways they seem to cancel out each other, so that the net result is zero! Many of these tensions leave me on a dead-end street. What's the profit under the sun, when you slice life across the middle and analyze all the strata, when you boil it down to its basics and put yourself into it at 86,400 seconds a day, there's zero in it for you." [Living On The Ragged Edge, by Charles R. Swindoll, p. 77]

Sometimes it seems like that! We went to H & R Block to have our taxes done. I was thrilled when the lady informed us that we were getting back over $300 from Federal. Then I was not quite as thrilled when she said we owed $90 to the State. As we got up to leave she said we could pay for her services at the desk – her 20 minute work cost $250! I now know how the fella felt when he sang, "The Thrill is gone!" Life is like that – if you leave God and eternity out of the picture you're doing good is you end up with zero. Don Anderson drives home the problem of a person who realizes that he is not in control of his life:

"The reality that his life is beyond his control may hit a man in mid-life hard, like a heavy weight boxer's punch to the belly. Not only does God dictate the movement of the years, but our family, friends, and career may seem to function independently too. His wife may begin to try her wings and return to school or the work force. His kids are probably typical teenagers who increasingly flaunt their independence...His boss fires, hires, transfers people, and generally operates without his consent...Frustrated by the out-of-control state of affairs he may begin to resent God's sovereignty...In fact one of the main reasons a severe crisis occurs in the life of an individual is because he's attempting to combat something that God has permitted in his life.

The fellow in crisis is increasingly dissatisfied with the circumstances in which the Lord has placed him...This unhappiness is really rebellion, resistance to God's will and the rub is that no matter how we resist, the Lord isn't going to budge till we break (Psa. 51:17)...Solomon has been looking for answers – he has fought, he has indulged, he has worked himself to a point of exhaustion; his marriages are in trouble, his job is a hassle, his kingdom is crumbling, he can find no real purpose or meaning in life. Everything he tries seems to end in failure." [Ecclesiastes The Mid-Life Crisis, by Don Anderson, pp. 81-82]

GOD'S SOVEREIGN WAYS ARE IN SECRET
God's Sovereign ways are *Unknown*
 He Reaffirms that God is Sovereign
 [11] He has made everything beautiful in its time – at least he understood this truth. Again he is going up for a gulp of needed air! He also realizes understanding God's sovereignty is Removed from those living under the

[12] sun.....*Also He has put eternity in their hearts, except that no one can find out the work that God does from beginning to end* [12] *I know that nothing is better for them than to rejoice, and to do good in their lives,* [13] *and also that every man should eat and drink and enjoy the good of all his labor--it is the gift of God* – those under the sun simply cannot make sense out of life.

God's sovereign ways are *Unchangeable*

I know that whatever God does, It shall be forever. Nothing can be added to it, And nothing taken from it. God does it, that men should fear before Him. [15] *That which is has already been, And what is to be has already been; And God requires an account of what is past* – we might as well sit back enjoy the ride because we are not in the driver's seat – God is!

* Nebuchadnezzar learned that truth - [16] "Let his mind be changed from *that of* a man And let a beast's mind be given to him, And let seven periods of time pass over him. [17] "This sentence is by the decree of the *angelic* watchers And the decision is a command of the holy ones, In order that the living may know That the Most High is ruler over the realm of mankind, And bestows it on whom He wishes And sets over it the lowliest of men." Daniel 4:16-17

* Job learned that, "[1] Then Job answered the LORD and said, [2] "I know that You can do all things, And that no purpose of Yours can be thwarted. [3] 'Who is this that hides counsel without knowledge?' "Therefore I have declared that which I did not understand, Things too wonderful for me, which I did not know." Job 42:1-3

* David knew this truth - [10] So David blessed the LORD in the sight of all the assembly; and David said, "Blessed are You, O LORD God of Israel our father, forever and ever. [11] "Yours, O LORD, is the greatness and the power and the glory and the victory and the majesty, indeed everything that is in the heavens and the earth; Yours is the dominion, O LORD, and You exalt Yourself as head over all. [12] "Both riches and honor *come* from You, and You rule over all, and in Your hand is power and might; and it lies in Your hand to make great and to strengthen everyone. 1 Chronicles 29:10-12

* Jehoshaphat got it — ⁵ Then Jehoshaphat stood in the assembly of Judah and Jerusalem, in the house of the LORD before the new court, ⁶ and he said, "O LORD, the God of our fathers, are You not God in the heavens? And are You not ruler over all the kingdoms of the nations? Power and might are in Your hand so that no one can stand against You. 2 Chronicles 20:5-6

Sooner or later we will learn this truth also! Tozer writes:

"God is not a railway porter who carries your suitcase and serves you. God is God. He made heaven and earth. He holds the world in His hand. He measures the dust of the earth in the balance. He spreads the sky out like a mantle. He is the great God Almighty. He is not your servant."

God's sovereignty seems to be *Unfair*

CONTEXT
¹⁶ *Moreover I saw under the sun:* - without a future judgment people seem to be getting away with murder.

CONFLICT
...In the place of judgment, Wickedness was there; And in the place of righteousness, Iniquity was there — injustice seems to reign unchallenged. Henry Longfellow familiar word ring all too true:

"I heard the bells on Christmas Day" his mind goes back to the promise of the angels saying, "Peace on earth, good will to men." But he simple doesn't find it, so he continues, "In despair I bowed my head, there is no peace on earth I said, for hate is strong and mocks the song of peace on earth."

CONFIDENCE
¹⁷ *I said in my heart, "God shall judge the righteous and the wicked, For there is a time there for every purpose and for every work."* – again he comes up for a brief gulp of air!

We can only take so much of this under the sun stuff before we are desperately searching for something from above.

A COMPARISON

Because men under the sun do not recognize God or eternity it seems like men die like animals.

Both man and beast Die

[18] I said in my heart, "Concerning the condition of the sons of men, God tests them, that they may see that they themselves are like animals." [19] For what happens to the sons of men also happens to animals; one thing befalls them: as one dies, so dies the other. Surely, they all have one breath; man has no advantage over animals, for all is vanity.

Both will then physically Deteriorate

[20] All go to one place: all are from the dust, and all return to dust.

Both will Desist and Disappear

[21] Who knows the spirit of the sons of men, which goes upward, and the spirit of the animal, which goes down to the earth? — from a merely physical observation you cannot see man's spirit leave his body.

Swindoll, "These words represent precisely how he felt at time of writing and exactly what he said, but they are no more representative of truth to live by than any other border line heresy found in a random sampling of any other similar section of scripture. Solomon has unwisely and rashly stated heresy. The inspiration of scripture guarantees that, that is indeed what he wrote. But discernment from the complete body of scriptural truth restrains us from blindly believing the same thing." [[Living On The Ragged Edge, by Charles R. Swindoll, p. 104].

The point is that if you leave God and eternity out of the picture there seems to be no distinction between the death of a man and his dog! This by the way is the natural conclusion of evolution! As one rightly noted, "If we are repulsed by such a low view of human existence, we should realize that it is but a natural extension of the atheistic theories of human origins. If the supernatural dimension is discounted, if we are confined to what we can deduce by ourselves from the world around us, a logical conclusion is that we have no higher beginning or ultimate purpose then do the animals with whom we share the earth."

An illogical Conclusion

²² So I perceived that nothing is better than that a man should rejoice in his own works, for that is his heritage. For who can bring him to see what will happen after him? – in other words try to find some joy in this life even though everything ends at the grave.

³²...If the dead do not rise, *"Let us eat and drink, for tomorrow we die!"* 1 Corinthians 15:32b

The Continuation of oppression

Why does God allow oppression to continue? Why doesn't He step in and put an end to it? He will, but those who leave God and eternity out of the picture do not see that day coming.

The Fact of oppression seems unfair

¹ Then I returned and considered all the oppression that is done under the sun: - the abuse of power is a fact of life.

Whether on the job, in schools, in the government, or society in general.

THE FEELINGS OF THE OPPRESSED
THEY ARE DISTRAUGHT
And look! The tears of the oppressed – they have a feeling of hopelessness; a sense of loss – loss of self-respect, security, of possessions and of life itself. As one cheer goes:

"Here's to those who love us
And here's to those who don't
A smile for those who are willing to,
And a tear for those who won't."

⁶ They attack, they lurk, They watch my steps, As they have waited *to take* my life. ⁷ Because of wickedness, cast them forth, In anger put down the peoples, O God! ⁸ You have taken account of my wanderings; Put my tears in Your bottle. Are *they* not in Your book? Psalm 56:6-8

THEY ARE DESTITUTE

But they have no comforter – when you're on top you have friends coming out of the woodwork; but when you hit rock bottom you feel like a door mat, trampled upon and left alone. I have learned those who are on top, think they can never be brought low; and those brought low, think they can never be on top again – both are wrong! As of this writing I'm on the bottom of the heap. No revivals; no new members; no converts; no faithfulness from most regular members; and support drying up...I lead the singing, do the preach- ing, read the Scriptures, and clean the church when I can. Friends are few but refuse to give up! And have found being reduced to the Lord Jesus in spite of my many failures, is an inner delight in the midst of outer destitution.

²⁰ Reproach has broken my heart and I am so sick. And I looked for sympathy, but there was none, And for comforters, but I found none. Psalm 69:20

² She weeps bitterly in the night And her tears are on her cheeks; She has none to comfort her Among all her lovers. All her friends have dealt treacherously with her; They have become her enemies. Lamentations 1:2

THEY ARE DISADVANTAGED

On the side of their oppressors there is power, But they have no comforter – people with position and money seems to fare better in our court system then others!

THEY ARE IN DESPAIR

²Therefore I praised the dead who were already dead, More than the living who are still alive. ³Yet, better than both is he who has never existed, Who has not seen the evil work that is done under the sun. ⁴Again, I saw that for all toil and every skillful work a man is envied by his neighbor. This also is vanity and grasping for the wind — Job felt the same way!

¹Afterward Job opened his mouth and cursed the day of his *birth.* ²And Job said, ³"Let the day perish on which I was to be born, And the night *which* said, 'A boy is conceived.' ⁴"May that day be darkness; Let not God above care for it, Nor light shine on it. ⁵"Let darkness and black gloom claim it; Let a cloud settle on it; Let the blackness of the day terrify it. ⁶"*As for* that night, let darkness seize it; Let it not rejoice among the days of the year; Let it not come into the number of the months.

⁷"Behold, let that night be barren; Let no joyful shout enter it. ⁸"Let those curse it who curse the day, Who are prepared to rouse Leviathan. ⁹"Let the stars of its twilight be darkened; Let it wait for light but have none, And let it not see the breaking dawn; ¹⁰Because it did not shut the opening of my *mother's* womb, Or hide trouble from my eyes. Job 3:1-10

¹⁷'You renew Your witnesses against me And increase Your anger toward me; Hardship after hardship is with me. ¹⁸'Why then have You brought me out of the womb? Would that I had died and no eye had seen me! ¹⁹'I should have been as though I had not been, Carried from womb to tomb.' Job 10:17-19

All of this reminded me of Frank Sinatra's song, *That's Life:*

"That's life, that's what people says,
   Your riding high in April, shot down in May...
   That's life, funny as it seems,
Some people get their kicks, step-en on dreams.
But I don't let it get me down,
Cause this old world keeps spinning around.
I've been a puppet, a pauper, pirate, a poet, a pawn and a king.

I've been up and down and over and out,
And I know one thing.

Each time I find myself flat on my face,
I just pick myself up and get back in the race.
That's life...

But then the song concludes:

"But if there's nothing shaking, coming this July. I'm gonna roll myself up, in a
big ball,
And die! My! My!

Vanity of life comes from not being able to figure out the ways of God. Since he
comes up for a gulp of air every now and then we need to also. Don Anderson led
a young man to the Lord. They became good friends. One day at the lake they
were pulling an inner tube behind a boat. This young man who had been saved
was having a blast hanging onto the inner tube and he was being pulled through
the waters. Suddenly the boat veered sharply and the man flew off – he hit a
stump and died instantly. He was only 22 years old and left behind a wife who was
pregnant with their second son. She obviously could not understand the ways that
God allows. Several months went by and Don asked her to sing a special at church.
  She did and the song she chose to sing with Through it all:

Verse 1:
I've had many tears and sorrows,
I've had questions for tomorrow,
there's been times I didn't know right from wrong.
But in every situation,
God gave me blessed consolation,
that my trials come to only make me strong.

Chorus:
Through it all,
through it all,
I've learned to trust in Jesus,
I've learned to trust in God.

Through it all,
through it all,
I've learned to depend upon His Word.

Verse 2:
I've been to lots of places,
I've seen a lot of faces,
there's been times I felt so all alone.
But in my lonely hours,
yes, those precious lonely hours,
Jesus lets me know that I was His own

Chorus

Verse 3:
I thank God for the mountains,
and I thank Him for the valleys,
I thank Him for the storms He brought me through.
For if I'd never had a problem,
I wouldn't know God could solve them,
I'd never know what faith in God could do.
André Crouch
[Ecclesiastes, The Mid-life Crisis, by Don Anderson, pp. 115-116]

CHAPTER 8

Without Love

§

(Without Companionship)

I awakened this morning, I was filled with despair
All my dreams turned to ashes and gone, oh yeah
As I looked at my life it was barren and bare
Without love I've had nothing at all
Without love I've had nothing
Without love I've had nothing at all
I have conquered the world
All but one thing did I have
Without love I've had nothing at all
Once I had a sweetheart who loved only me
There was nothing, oh that she would not give, oh no
But I was blind to her goodness and I could not see
That a heart without love cannot live
Without love I've had nothing
Without love I've had nothing at all
I have conquered the world
All but one thing did I have
Without love I've had nothing at all
[Recorded: 1969/01/23, first released on Back in Memphis (From Memphis to Vegas)]

TEACHER: ⁴THEN I SAW YET another thing: envy fuels achievement. All the
work and skills people develop come from their desire to be better than their

neighbors. Even this is fleeting, like trying to embrace the wind. [5]As the saying goes: The fool folds his hands to rest and lets his flesh waste away. [6]And it is better to have one handful of peace than to have two hands full of hard work and a desire to catch the wind.

[7]Again I observed another example of how fleeting life is under the sun: [8]a person who is all alone— with no child, no sibling— yet he works hard his entire life. Still he is never satisfied with the wealth he gains. Does he stop to ask, "Why am I working so hard?" or "Why am I depriving myself of life's simple pleasures?" This, too, is fleeting, like trying to catch hold of a breath; it's a miserable situation. [9]Two are better than one because a good return comes when two work together. [10]If one of them falls, the other can help him up. But who will help the pitiful person who falls down alone? [11]In the same way, if two lie down together, they can keep each other warm. But how will the one who sleeps alone stay warm against the night? [12]And if one person is vulnerable to attack, two can drive the attacker away. As the saying goes, "A rope made of three strands is not quickly broken." [13]A poor, wise youth is better off than an old, foolish king who no longer accepts advice. [14]For example, once a young man marched out of prison to become king; it had not mattered how poor he once had been in his kingdom. [15]I saw all those who live out their lives under the sun flock to the side of a second youth who took the king's place. [16]There seemed to be no limit to all the people who were under his authority. Yet those who will come later will not be happy with him and will refuse to follow him. Even this, you see, is fleeting— power and influence do not last— like trying to pursue the wind. [Nelson, Thomas (2012-04-10). The Voice Bible: Step Into the Story of Scripture (pp. 773-774). Thomas Nelson. Kindle Edition.]

Novelist, essayist, and farmer Wendell Berry came across a plot of Maximilian Sunflowers, a nearly ten-foot tall plant native to the Midwest. One particular plant that was growing alone, disconnected from the "community" of other sunflowers. Wendell Berry observed that although this solo, individualistic plant had grown very tall, it was clearly not healthy. The blossoms were thick and heavy, so heavy that the branches were starting to strain and break under the weight. Berry noted that "In one sense the plant had "succeeded" as a solo plant. After all, it was growing and it was unusually tall. But, unfortunately, it had completely failed its intended purpose as a Maximilian Sunflower: these plants only thrive and give life as they grow in community, not in isolation. We could say that [achieving success solely] as an individual *was* the [plant's] failure. It had failed because it had lived outside an important part of its definition, which consists of individuality *and* its community. A part of its [healthy] potential lay in its community, not [just] itself." Man was never meant to live solely alone – even in the garden, in a perfect environment, with a sinless man, God said, "It is not good for man to live alone." The Vanity in life is intensified when we live Without companionship.

THE *MANAGER* WITHOUT COMPANIONSHIP 4:4-6

This manager is a Competitor. He is Dominated by his work. *Again, I saw that for all toil* – the word toil means "to engage in heavy, all-consuming labor." It pictures one who is completely devoted to his work. It is a priority that consumes all of his time and energy. He is what we call a workaholic. Rock star, David Byrne, is co-founder of The Talking Heads, and a Golden Globe and Academy Award winner said: "I think I might be a workaholic. A lot of it is a way of dealing with other parts of living that I don't feel as comfortable with, such as relating with human beings. He is also Distinguished. Notice, *and every skillful work* – this word speaks of one "who is successful and prosperous in an endeavor." Since he has given himself completely over to his work, he has become good at what he does. He is Disliked, *a man is envied by his neighbor* – TWOT, "The verb expresses a very strong emotion in a derogatory sense, denotes hostility and disruptive passion. It may be helpful to think of this word as a zeal for another's property or status." Like Josephs brothers who hated him because of his success (Gen. 37:11). Wrath *is* cruel and anger a torrent, But who *is* able to stand before jealousy? Proverbs 27:4 Then he is Dissatisfied, the familiar *This also is vanity and grasping for the wind* – he can live with those who dislike him, he even expects it. But what's hard to take is the fact that in spite of all his hard work he is not satisfied. A 2006 study of 1,733 executives asked the question: "If you could start your career over in a completely different field, would you?"

Yes—51 percent
Maybe—24 percent

No—25 percent
In other words 75% were not really satisfied.

Judist Viorst:

"I've finished six pillows in Needlepoint,
And I'm reading Jane Austen and Kant,
And I'm up to the pork with black beans, in Advanced Chinese cooking.
I don't have to struggle to find myself.
For I already know what I want,
I want to be healthy and wise and extremely good looking.

I'm learning new glazes in pottery class,
And I'm playing new chords in Guitar,
And in Yoga I'm starting to master the *lotus* position.

I don't have to ponder priorities,
For I already know what they are:
To be good-looking, healthy and wise.

I'm improving my serve with a tennis pro,
And I'm practicing verb forms in Greek,
And in Pri*mal* Scream Therapy all my frustrations are vented.
I don't have to ask what I'm searching for
Since I already know, what I seek.
To be good-looking, healthy and wise.
And adored. And contented.

I've bloomed Organic Gardening,
And in dance I have tightened my thighs,
And in Conscientious Raising,
There's no one around who can top me.

And I'm working all day and I'm working all night,
To be good-looking, healthy, and wise.
And adored. And contented. And brave. And well-read...

Won't someone, please, stop me!"

This manager is not Complacent. Here we have extremes – at least the worka-holic can say that he is not just sitting around doing nothing. He is not Stupid. He refers to *the fool,* the complacent are stupid or silly. He is not Slothful, it says *folds his hand,* meaning that he has no ambition to work. He is in fact lazy and irresponsibility. Today we are an entitlement society. I read an article this past week that noted: "A higher percentage of the American population is receiving government benefits than ever before... Yes, we should always have a "safety net", but right now our "safety net" is becoming massively overloaded as millions more Americans jump on to it every single year.

The following are 16 statistics which show that the number of Americans dependent on the government is at an all-time high....

#1 According to the Census Bureau, <u>49 percent</u> of all Americans live in a home that gets direct monetary benefits from the federal government. Back in 1983, <u>less than a third</u> of all Americans lived in a home that received direct monetary benefits from the federal government.

#2 The amount of money that the federal government gives directly to Americans has increased <u>by 32 percent</u> since Barack Obama entered the White House.

#3 The number of Americans receiving Social Security disability benefits has increased <u>by 10 percent</u> since Barack Obama first took office.

#4 Back in 1990, the federal government accounted for <u>32 percent</u> of all health care spending in America. Today, that figure is up to <u>45 percent</u> and it is projected to surpass <u>50 percent</u> very shortly.

#5 The number of Americans on food stamps recently hit a new all-time high. It has increased by <u>3 million</u> since this time last year and by more than 14 million since Barack Obama first entered the White House.

#6 Today, one out of every seven Americans is on food stamps and <u>one out of every four</u> American children is on food stamps. This is unprecedented in American history.

#7 In 2010, <u>42 percent</u> of all single mothers in the United States were on food stamps.

#8 Back in 1980, government transfer payments accounted for just<u>11.7%</u> of all income. In 2010, government transfer payments accounted for 18.4% of all income, which was a new all-time high.

#9 By the end of 2011, approximately 55 million Americans received a total of approximately <u>727 billion dollars</u> in Social Security benefits. As the <u>retirement crisis</u> becomes much worse, that dollar figure is projected to absolutely skyrocket.

#10 According to the Congressional Budget Office, the Social Security system <u>paid out more in benefits than it received in payroll taxes</u> in 2010. That was not supposed to happen until at least 2016.

#11 Back in 1965, only one out of every 50 Americans was on Medicaid. Today, <u>one out of every 6</u> Americans is on Medicaid, and things are about to get a whole lot worse. It is being projected that Obamacare will add <u>16 million more Americans</u> to the Medicaid rolls.

#12 The U.S. government now says that the Medicare trust fund will run out <u>five years faster</u> than previously anticipated.

#13 The total cost of just three federal government programs - the Department of Defense, Social Security and Medicare - exceeded the total amount of taxes brought in during fiscal 2010 <u>by 10 billion dollars</u>.

#14 It is being projected that entitlement spending by the federal government <u>will nearly double</u> by the year 2050.

#15 Right now, spending by the federal government accounts for about <u>24 percent</u> of GDP. Back in 2001, it accounted for just 18 percent.

#16 When you total it all up, American households are now receiving more money directly from the federal government <u>than they are paying to the government in taxes</u>.

Again, he is not Suicidal. The words, *And consumes his own flesh* — the complacent are like a man cutting his own heart out and eating it for lunch!

The Workaholic is not complacent. This is to his credit but as we shall see, he still is not satisfied. This manager is also not Contented either. It says, *Better a handful with quietness Than both hands full, together with toil and grasping for the wind* – here is an appeal for balance! Contentment comes from being Responsible. One handful – is the right approach. If you have two handfuls you are overcommitted; if you have empty hands you are irresponsible. Contentment brings Rest. Quietness – a peaceful inner rest. This is something both the workaholic and the bum lack. Contentment comes from Restraint. Both hands full – is obviously a picture of over commitment. A contented person learns the value of saying no! The manager who is a driven competitor is never complacent. But he is never truly contented either. Why? Because if we leave God out nothing is ever enough! We will have a greedy grasping spirit for more – but nothing but God can satisfy that desire.

Stowell noted, "Several years ago, [my wife] and I moved out of Chicago to the western suburbs to be near our grandkids. We got this little piece of land and built what we thought was our dream house. It was not over the top by any means, but it was nice. We liked how it looked from the curb. We liked how it lived on the inside. It was far more than we deserved, but we really liked our house. I hate to admit this ... but about six months after we built our house, I was driving through a beautiful neighborhood and saw a house that caught my attention.

The colors, the architecture, the lot, the location all had a big wow factor for me. And my first thought was, *Boy, do I wish I had that house!* Have you ever wondered, *What is wrong with us?* It's the Eve factor in our lives. We were born with it, and it's deeply embedded in our spiritual DNA. Just one more proof of our sinfulness, in case we had forgotten. What was it that drew Eve's heart away from God in Genesis 3? What was it that seduced her into the material world, into Satan's clutches? She wanted more. What she had, although awesome and satisfying, wasn't enough. In fact, for her, God wasn't enough. She was willing to do anything for more, even if it meant turning her back on God. At its core, greed is a lack of contentment with God and with what he has provided for us."

THE *MISER* WHO IS WITHOUT COMPANIONSHIP. 4:7-12

He is a successful man with no Friends, note [7] *Then I returned, and I saw vanity under the sun:* [8] *There is one alone, without companion:* - lit. "without a second." He has no business partner; no associate; no close companion. It is the Lone Ranger without Tonto; Laural without Hardy; Andy Griffith without

Barney; Mat Dillon without Kitty; Sanford without son; He has no Family, He has neither son nor brother — he is too busy to have a family. If he is married having children cost too much! He has no Future. *Yet there is no end to all his labors, Nor is his eye satisfied with riches. But he never asks, "For whom do I toil and deprive myself of good?" This also is vanity and a grave misfortune* — there is no one to leave all his stuff with. He feels like Abraham who said, "Lord what will you give me, seeing I go childless?" (Gen. 15:2). He is also missing something Fabulous. 9-12:

- Companions bring Productivity. [9] *Two are better than one, Because they have a good reward for their labor* — this is just common sense!
- Companions bring Provision. 10-11 [10] *For if they fall, one will lift up his companion. But woe to him who is alone when he falls, For he has no one to help him up.* [11] *Again, if two lie down together, they will keep warm; But how can one be warm alone?* Garrett, "The warmth of lying beside each other does not refer to sexual activity, nor are the two necessarily husband and wife. It is an image derived from that of travelers who must lie beside each other to stay warm on cold desert nights. But the usage is here metaphorical for emotional comfort against the coldness of the world." The Misers money will do little to keep him warm as he faces the chill of life!
- Companions bring Protection. 12 [12] *Though one may be overpowered by another, two can withstand him. And a threefold cord is not quickly broken* — we might think of David and Jonathan. Read 1 Sam. 19-20 Jonathan often protected David against his father Saul.

Companionship is a good and needed thing which the Miser in his foolish greed does not comprehend. And we are not talking about patsy but real friends who tell us the truth when we need it. I remember reading that when Elvis was getting ready to do a special, Aloha From Hawaii, a man looked Elvis straight in the eye and said, "Elvis your way overweight!" Elvis took off his sunglasses, threw them across the room and headed for the man. He gave him a hug and said, "Thanks, for telling me the truth!"

THE *MONARCH* WITHOUT COMPANIONSHIP 13-16

Louis Goldberg: "The description of a king who has grown old and out of touch with the needs of his people (v.13). He has come to enjoy the benefits of rulership, he is taken up with those around him who cater to his every whim and pleasure. But the person has become old and senile, no longer able to rule effectively and even allowing the government to become corrupt. This brings discontentment and along comes a young man who takes over to clean-up the government with his administration (v. 14). This young man can identify with the needs of the people. This king starts out well (15-16a), but as time goes by he gets old also, a new generation comes on the scene and the king is then rejected (16b). The tragedy is nothing is learned by the previous experience and the process will repeat itself over and over again."

Perhaps if the Monarch would surround himself with true companions, who would tell him the truth, things would change? Vanity of life is intensified when we live without companionship. The fact is, all many have, is a Face-book Friendship's which really is no friendship is at all!

In a *New York Times* magazine article, Hal Niedzviecki reflected on social media sites—specifically, Facebook. Soon after starting a Facebook account, Hal had accumulated about 700 on-line "friends." In his own words, he was "absurdly proud of how many cyber pals, connections, acquaintances, and even strangers I'd managed to sign up." But he went on to point out that due to a 2-year-old at home, his "workaholic irritability," even his love of being left alone, he had fewer in-the-flesh friends to hang out with than he'd ever had before. So he decided to have a Facebook party to push his virtual friends into actual friends. Hal invited all 700 of his "friends" to a local bar for a party. People could respond to one of three options: "Attending," "Maybe Attending" and "Not Attending." Fifteen said they would be there, and sixty said they might be there. He guessed somewhere around 20 would show up. He writes about what happened next: "On the evening in question, I took a shower. I shaved.

I splashed on my tingly man perfume. I put on new pants and a favorite shirt. Brimming with optimism, I headed over to the neighborhood watering hole and waited. And waited. And waited. Eventually, one person showed up." And the one woman who showed up to meet Niedzviecki? He didn't know her. She was a friend of a friend. They ended up making small talk and then she left. Hal waited till midnight but no one else showed up. So, he ordered a beer and sulked. He concludes his article with these words: "Seven hundred friends, and I was drinking alone."

The Walls have ears

§

(Worthless Words)

The walls have ears, ears that hear each little sound you make
Every time you stamp through a lamp and every cup and dish you break
But they can't hear a kiss or two arms that hold you tight
So come on baby, don't fight tonight
The walls have ears, better think before you fling that shoe
If you part my hair with a chair, they'll spread the news to Timbuktu
But they can't hear a kiss or two arms that hold you tight
So come on baby, don't fight tonight
Jets can fly, fast and high, rockets can go even faster
But they can't catch or even match sound traveling through plaster
The walls have ears, ears that hear each little sound you make
Every time you stamp through a lamp and every cup and dish you break
But they can't hear a kiss or two arms that hold you tight
So come on baby, don't fight tonight Just in tonight
Don't fight tonight
[Recorded: 1962/03/27, first released on Girls! Girls! Girls!]

Dave McLaughlin, "I was at a bagpipe competition—yes, I'm Scottish—and I
expected the judges to be fans of bagpipe music. *So why,* I wondered, *did they have
their hands over their ears?* Inflated bagpipes naturally make a steady droning noise.
The actual music is played over and above that. In covering their ears the judges

shut out some of the low pitched noise while still hearing the higher pitched melody. Low level noise surrounds us wherever we go, whether it's the rumble of traffic or the incessant inane chatter coming from the television. But a lot of it comes out of our mouths. Imagine if every word you spoke in a day were laid out for a judge to examine by the standard of usefulness or [effectiveness]. How many of them would be deemed offensive or simply unnecessary noise?" It's frightening to think that an Omniscient God hears every trivial, obnoxious, thoughtless word we let spill from our mouths. Let's make sure he doesn't feel like covering his ears when we open our pipes. The vanity of life comes from our Worthless Words (Eccless. 5:1-9).

WORTHLESS WORDS ARE UNPROTECTED WORDS

THE CONCEPT

Walk prudently – lit. "keep your foot." It means "to exercise great care." Worthless words come when we talk before we think about what we are going to say. The word "walk" is usually a reference to one's behavior, but is in this context related to words...vv. 2,3,6,7.

THE CONTEXT

when you go to the house of God – the house of God can be related to the Temple or the synagogue. But by application is referring to whenever we come into God's presence. We need to Think before we Talk!

[3] He who guards his mouth preserves his life, *But* he who opens wide his lips shall have destruction. Proverbs 13:3

[20] Do you see a man hasty in his words? *There is* more hope for a fool than for him. Proverbs 29:20

[19] So then, my beloved brethren, let every man be swift to hear, slow to speak, slow to wrath; James 1:19

Robin Pearson shared, "I was swamped with calls in the church office. A woman requested the address of a missionary in Africa. I put her on hold while I looked for it. Just then the phone rang again. On that line, a mother asked for housing ideas for her wayward daughter. I asked her to hold while I got back to the first woman. A bit flustered, I accidentally picked up the second line. You can imagine that mother's surprise when I rattled off the African address for her wayward daughter! No telling how much misinformation we give out when we do not think carefully before we speak. Spurgeon, "I believe a very large majority of churchgoers are merely unthinking, slumbering worshipers of an unknown God."

WORTHLESS WORDS DO NOT *PAY* ATTENTION TO GOD'S WORD

The Arrogance, *and draw near to hear rather than to give the sacrifice of fools-* we should come into God's presence with the idea of responding to what He has to say, not to arrogantly tell Him what needs to be done!

> [8] Then he waited seven days, according to the time set by Samuel. But Samuel did not come to Gilgal; and the people were scattered from him. [9] So Saul said, "Bring a burnt offering and peace offerings here to me." And he offered the burnt offering. [10] Now it happened, as soon as he had finished presenting the burnt offering, that Samuel came; and Saul went out to meet him, that he might greet him. [11] And Samuel said, "What have you done?" And Saul said, "When I saw that the people were scattered from me, and *that* you did not come within the days appointed, and *that* the Philistines gathered together at Michmash, [12] then I said, 'The Philistines will now come down on me at Gilgal, and I have not made supplication to the LORD.' Therefore I felt compelled, and offered a burnt offering."

> [13] And Samuel said to Saul, "You have done foolishly. You have not kept the commandment of the LORD your God, which He commanded you. For now the LORD would have established your kingdom over Israel forever. 1 Samuel 13:8-13

Saul was foolish in not listening to God, who had limited offering sacrifices by way of the Priest. How many come to worship God singing Frank Sinatra's song, My Way.

"I planned each charted course,
each careful step along the byway,
And more, much more than this, I did it my way."

"My Way," made the Top 30 in 1969. Sinatra himself said that "My Way" became his "national anthem." Someone has said, "It's the national anthem of hell!" The lyrics were written by Paul Anka, and has been recorded by more than 100 artists in the first few years of its release. Former Soviet leader Mikhail Gorbachev was referring to this song when he said that the "Sinatra Doctrine" should replace the "Brezhnev Doctrine" for the Soviet satellite countries to be allowed to control their own destinies.

As one notes, "The song appeals to our prideful desire to be totally in charge. We have a tendency to wrest control from God, often without realizing it. This is perhaps the reason God listed as the first commandment, "You must not have any other god but me" (Exodus 20:3). This is probably the one commandment we violate most frequently— the "other god" most often being ourselves." When we live under the sun, we have no choice but to live our way instead of God's way.

[26]He who trusts in his own heart is a fool, But whoever walks wisely will be delivered. Proverbs 28:26

The Ignorance, *for they do not know that they do evil* – this is ignorance. "The term, *evil* carries the idea of something disastrous and painful, not of moral failure and evil. Therefore the fool here is not doing something morally outrageous but stupid." [A Handbook on Ecclesiastes, Ogden and Zogo]

We rarely think of evil as being ignorance of God. We think evil has to be some violent crime or sexual failure or something. But evil is simple being willfully ignorant of God. You would think we would not need to warn people of the ignorance of not paying attention to God. But why not, the world is full of warnings that are for fools. The following warnings are actually found on consumer products:

- On a Dura flame fireplace log: "Caution—Risk of Fire."
- On a Batman costume: "Warning: Cape does not enable user to fly."

* On a bottle of hair coloring: "Do not use as an ice cream topping."
* On a cardboard sun shield for a car: "Do not drive with sun shield in place."
* On a portable stroller: "Caution: Remove infant before folding for storage."

WORTHLESS WORDS ARE INAPPROPRIATE IN PRAYER
THEY LACKED RESTRAINT

Prayer is offered from a Thoughtless Mind. We are warned, *Do not be rash with your mouth* – again if we would think before we would talk, we would not say many of the things we say. It happens to the best of us! Two influential preachers, Charles Spurgeon and Joseph Parker, occupied pulpits in London during the 19th century. On one occasion, Parker commented about the poor condition of children admitted to Spurgeon's orphanage. It was reported to Spurgeon, however, that Parker had criticized the orphanage itself. The next Sunday Spurgeon blasted Parker from his pulpit. That attack, printed in the newspaper, became the talk of the town. Later Spurgeon got the whole story and apologized to Parker.

[29] Then the Spirit of the LORD came upon Jephthah, and he passed through Gilead and Manasseh, and passed through Mizpah of Gilead; and from Mizpah of Gilead he advanced *toward* the people of Ammon. [30] And Jephthah made a vow to the LORD, and said, "If You will indeed deliver the people of Ammon into my hands, [31]then it will be that whatever comes out of the doors of my house to meet me, when I return in peace from the people of Ammon, shall surely be the LORD'S, and I will offer it up as a burnt offering." Judges 11:29-31

[34] When Jephthah came to his house at Mizpah, there was his daughter, coming out to meet him with timbrels and dancing; and she *was his* only child. Besides her he had neither son nor daughter. [35] And it came to pass, when he saw her, that he tore his clothes, and said, "Alas, my daughter! You have brought me very low! You are among those who trouble me! For I have given my word to the LORD, and I cannot go back on it."

Judges 11:34-35

Prayer offered from a Talkative Mouth. *And let not your heart utter anything hastily before God...* [3] *For a dream comes through much activity, And a fool's voice is known by his many words* – we talk too much, especially in prayer!

⁷ And when you pray, do not use vain repetitions as the heathen *do*. For they think that they will be heard for their many words. Matthew 6:7

John Climacus, "Let all multiplicity be absent from your prayer. A single word was enough for the publican and the prodigal son to receive God's pardon...Do not try to find exactly the right words for your prayer: how many times does the simple and monotonous stuttering of children draw the attention of their father! Do not launch into long discourses, for if you do, your mind will be dissipated trying to find just the right words. The publican's short sentence moved God to mercy. A single word full of faith saved the thief."

¹⁹ In the multitude of words sin is not lacking, But he who restrains his lips *is* wise. Proverbs 10:19

I can think of only one time when a multitude of words were helpful. On October 14, 1912, Theodore Roosevelt was saved by his many words. Roosevelt had just served one term as president, and was running for the office again. As he left his hotel in Milwaukee on that day, he stuffed his thick, wordy campaign speech in his breast pocket. He was confronted by a gun-toting bartender. The bullet did crack one of Roosevelt's ribs, but the thickness of his speech probably saved him from death.

But more often a multitude of words gets us into trouble, Jean Paul Sartre once said,

"Words are loaded pistols." Consider this: The Lord's Prayer contains 56 words; the Gettysburg Address, 266; the Ten Commandments, 297; the Declaration of Independence, 300; and a recent U.S. government order setting the price of cabbage, 26,911.

THE REASON

For God is in heaven, and you on earth — must remember that we are addressing Deity!

Hubbard, "Babbling, rambling, wild words may be all right in dreams, but they do not belong in worship. Our relationship to God is one of sober, respectful, reverent awe. False worship is as much an affront to Him as obscene insults are to a wife or husband. Better to bribe a judge then to ply God with hollow words; better to slap a policeman than to seek God's influence by meaningless gestures."

THE REQUIREMENT

Therefore let your words be few- better to speak just a few words that are right, then a multitude that are wrong. Louie and Jeanette, a couple in their 80s, have a 55-year-old son, Louis. Their son has been severely mentally handicapped all his life. As Christian parents, Louie and Jeanette were concerned about their son's spiritual development and prayed for him often. Their son only speaks an occasional short phrase or a few isolated words at a time, so there was no way to know if he understood anything about Christ. About the time Louis was 50 years old, an amazing thing happened. The family was together on a car ride when, all of a sudden, without warning or prompting, Louis began to speak. He said, "You know Mom, you know Dad, Jesus was born, Jesus died to save us from our sins. He rose again, yes he did." These are the only complete sentences they have ever heard from their son. Better to be like Louis then to spew out a multitude of foolish words.

WORTHLESS WORDS ARE UNFULFILLED PROMISES

PAY UP.

[4] *When you make a vow to God, do not delay to pay it; For He has no pleasure in fools. Pay what you have vowed* – if we make a vow then we should follow through. C. S. Lewis was determined to pay what he had vowed. His biography tells of the suffering he endured because he kept a promise he had made to a buddy during World War I. This friend was worried about the care of his wife and small daughter if he should be killed in battle, so Lewis assured him that if that were to happen he would look after them. As the war dragged on, the man was killed. True to his word, Lewis took care of his friend's family. Yet no matter how helpful he tried to be, the woman was ungrateful, rude, arrogant, and domineering. Through it all, Lewis kept forgiving her. He refused to let her actions become an excuse to renege on his promise.

OR SHUT UP.

[5] *Better not to vow than to vow and not pay* – probably the best thing to do is not to vow at all! Application Bible, "Solomon warns his readers about making foolish promises to God. In Israelite culture, making vows was a serious matter. Vows

were voluntary, but once made, they were unbreakable (<u>Deuteronomy 23:21-23</u>). It is foolish to make a vow you cannot keep or to play games with God by only partially fulfilling your vow (<u>Proverbs 20:25</u>). It's better not to vow than to make a vow to God and break it. If you make a vow, keep it."

LEST GOD'S ANGER FLARES-UP.

⁶ *Do not let your mouth cause your flesh to sin, nor say before the messenger of God that it was an error. Why should God be angry at your excuse and destroy the work of your hands?* – The messenger of God here refers to the priest. Most of the time we don't need to make promises to God or anyone else. But if we make them we should keep them!

Booker T. Washington tells the true story about a slave. Several years before the Emancipation Proclamation he made a deal with his master. In those days slaves were permitted to buy themselves. A slave, if the master permitted, could go off to work and send the master the money he earned, until he bought his freedom. This particular slave lived in Ohio and was working to buy his freedom from his master. When the Emancipation Proclamation freed him, he still owed his master 300 dollars. Technically he was free but continued to pay his master.

He said, "I have never broken a promise in my life. I could not enjoy my freedom until that debt us fulfilled." What a contrast with this generation! Just watch Judge Judy and you see case after case where people seem to think that contracts they signed do not need to be honored because it would inconvenience them. I have heard people say over and over again, "I don't have to pay because he or she co-signed." Lewis Smedes says:

"Yes, somewhere people still make and keep promises. They choose not to quit when the going gets rough because they promised once to see it through. They stick to lost causes. They hold on to a love grown cold. They stay with people who have become pains in the neck. They still dare to make promises and care enough to keep the promises they make. I want to say to you that if you have a ship you will not desert, if you have people you will not forsake, if you have causes you will not abandon, then you are like God. What a marvelous thing a promise is! When a person makes a promise, she reaches out into an unpredictable future and makes one thing predictable: she will be there even when being there costs her more than she wants to pay. When a person makes a promise, he stretches himself out into circumstances that no one can control and controls at least one thing: he will be there no matter what the circumstances turn out to be. With one simple word of promise, a person creates an island of certainty in a sea of uncertainty."

WORTHLESS WORDS DO NOT *PROPERLY* REVERENCE GOD
[7] For in the multitude of dreams and many words there is also vanity. But fear God – Prov. 1:7

This is the secret to life – fear God! If we fear God we will be careful about what we say. Six-year-old Angie and her four-year-old brother Joel were sitting together in church. Joel giggled, sang, and talked out loud. Finally, his big sister had had enough. "You're not supposed to talk out loud in church." "Why? Who's going to stop me?" Joel asked. Angie pointed to the back of the church and said, "See those two men standing by the door? They're hushers." The fear of God is like a husher that keeps us from being disrespectful to Almighty God. Bottom line is worthless words at best are worthless! The state of Washington has a significant percentage of citizens with Chinese or Korean ancestry. As Secretary of State, Sam Reed hoped to reach out to them in their own language. His messages to taxpayers were translated into Chinese and Korean on the state's website. Unfortunately, the translations didn't communicate as Reed intended.

When Reed wrote about "statewide mandates to restore public trust," the version posted in Chinese read: "Swampy weed suggests whole state order recover open trust." The Secretary of State's office pulled the translations, saying, "If it's totally confusing, it's worthless."

CHAPTER 10
Who needs money?

§

(Trying to find satisfaction in Wealth)

I'm on the right track for lots of kissin'
So that old greenback, I won't be missin'
All the greatest things in life are free
Who needs money, not me

Cash or credit, it doesn't matter
Long as my bank books keep growin' fatter
Easy street is my favorite avenue
Who needs money, I do

Just pity all those millionaires they never can relax
Because they're always worryin' about their income tax
Why waste time on high financin', I'd rather spend it on good romancin'
What if my pockets are empty as can be
Who needs money, not me
Tell me about it

Some folks save it, some folks lend it
But as for me I want to spend it
Give me some green and my skies will be blue
Who needs money, I do

Stocks and bonds, they only bore me
Interest holds no interest for me

Who wants to sit in the lap of luxury
Who needs money, not me

When I go to bed at night instead of counting sheep
I start counting dollar bills and then I fall asleep

Making money never thrills me
It's making love that really kills me
What can I lose with my philosophy

Who needs money, not me
What do you want

I want a big yacht, I can cruise in
The kind that girls just can't refuse in
All it takes is a million or two
Who needs money, I do

Any time some gal starts flirtin'
Now that I'm broke I know for certain
She really digs my personality
Tell me, who needs money not me

Poverty's the only thing that money cannot buy

So rich or poor it pays to have M-O-N-E-Y

A gal who's tender, that's what I love

It's legal tender, I want a pile of
Just let my liquid assets overflow

You can't take it with you when you go
So, who needs money

That lovely, lovely money

Who needs money, not me

[Recorded: 1967/02/22, first released on Clambake]

THE STORY IS TOLD OF a father of a wealthy family who took his son on a trip to the country to show his son how poor people can be. They spent a couple of days and nights on the farm of what would be considered a very poor family. On their return from the trip, the father asked his son, "How was the trip?" He said, "It was great, Dad." His father asked, "Did you see how poor people can be?" Son replied, "Oh yeah," Father asked, "So what did you learn from the trip?" The son answered: "I saw that we have one dog, and they have four. We have a pool that reaches to the middle of our garden, and they have a creek that has no end. We have a small piece of land to live on, and they have fields that go beyond sight. We buy our food, but they grow theirs." With this, the boy's father was speechless. Then his son added, "Thanks, Dad, for showing me how poor we are."

Those who focus only of material wealth are poor indeed. The frustration in life is we think material wealth is what would make us happy. We soon learn it is not! The Vanity of life is seen in trying to find satisfaction in Wealth (Eccles. 5:8-6:12)

WEALTH DOES GIVE AN ADVANTAGE IN *SOCEITY*. 5:8-9
If you see the oppression of the poor, and the violent perversion of justice and righteousness in a province, do not marvel at the matter; for high official watches over high official, and higher officials are over them. ⁹ Moreover the profit of the land is for all; even the king is served from the field – this is a complicated passage – but the bottom line is

"Officials have an unfair advantage to attain wealth." [MacArthur Study Bible]. And that wealth gives them obvious advantages.

Wealth can be used to oppress poor people and get ahead in this world. It has been rightly said, "It takes money to make money." But getting ahead in society means nothing when one comes to the end of their life.

Robert Ringer wrote, "In my early 20s I was introduced to Harold Hart, whose Wall Street investing had made him a millionaire. One evening I visited Mr. Hart to do a deal. When I arrived I found him resting in his favorite chair, with servants waiting on him hand and foot. I sat there waiting as he stared blankly into space. Finally he muttered, "You know, nature has played a great hoax on man. You work all your life, go through an endless number of struggles, play all the petty little games, and if you're lucky you finally make it to the top. Well I made it a long time ago, and you know what? It doesn't mean a damn thing. Nature's made a fool of man and the biggest fool of all is me. Here I sit, in poor health, exhausted from years of playing the game, well aware that time is running out, and I keep asking myself, 'Now what, genius? What's your next brilliant move going to be?' All that time I spent worrying, maneuvering—it was meaningless. Life is nothing but a big hoax. We think we're so important, but the truth is, we're nothing."

WEALTHY DOES NOT *SATISFY*. 5:10-11

THE PROBLEMS, ONE IS THAT OF *GREED*

[10] *He who loves silver will not be satisfied with silver; Nor he who loves abundance, with increase. This also is vanity-* greed cannot be satisfied!

[10] He who loves money shall never have enough. The foolishness of thinking that wealth brings happiness!

Ecclesiastes 5:10 (TLB)

John D Rockefeller was once asked, "How much money does it take to satisfy a man?" He answered, "Just a little bit more." He once said, "I have made many millions, but they have brought me no happiness. I would rather barter them all for the days I sat on an office stool in Cleveland and counted myself rich on $3 dollars a week."

THEN THERE IS THE PROBLEM OF *GOD*

[1] There is an evil which I have seen under the sun, and it is common among men: [2] A man to whom God has given riches and wealth and honor, so that he lacks nothing for himself of all he desires; yet God does not give him power to eat of it, but a foreigner consumes it. This is vanity, and it is an evil affliction – God doesn't honor greed!

"[2] There are people, for instance, on whom God showers everything—money, property, reputation—all they ever wanted or dreamed of. And then God doesn't let them enjoy it..." Ecclesiastes 6:2 (MSG)

America has clearly rejected God and as a result God has seen to it that people do not even recognize the prosperity that they have.

Affluenza is an hour-long PBS documentary which begins with a look at car commercials from the 1950s. The narrator says, "Are you old enough to remember the '50's—that golden age of prosperity following the Second World War?" Scenes of a prosperous family in the 1950s are shown as the narrator continues: "We felt richer then than we do now." The famous book at the time was *America: The Affluent Society.*" New York psychologist Paul Wachtel comments:

"[That book's] title would be laughable today. People would reject it. Even though we have actually in terms of gross national product more than twice as much. Everybody's home has got twice as much stuff in it." A number of scenes compare homes from the 1950s with modern homes. The narrator says, "Back in 1958, only 4 percent of American homes had dishwashers. Now more than half do; Less than 1 percent had color television. Now it's 97 percent; there were no microwaves, VCRs, or personal computers." The narrator continues: "Never enough. So much stuff. So little space, even though the average new house has grown larger every decade. Now many new homes have three-car garages. Nearly 900 square feet of garage space alone, which is about the size of an entire home in the 1950s." Ford commercials from the 1950s are compared with footage of modern cars. The narrator says, "In that gilded new world, hardly any new cars had air conditioning. Today more than 90 percent do. Economy cars, offer more features now, than luxury cars did then." A 1950s Chevrolet commercial is shown while the narrator says, "Just as they did in the '50's, new cars help us keep up with the Joneses. But these days we find it more appealing to fly. We fly 25 times as much as we did then." The point is, what they had back in the 50's is nothing compared to the wealth and advances that we have today – yet they considered themselves rolling in wealth, while most today view themselves as broke and disadvantaged! The big difference between the 50s and today – they had an awareness and gratitude toward God that is rarely found today...

THE PARASITES

[11] *When goods increase, They increase who eat them; So what profit have the owners Except to see them with their eyes?* - More taxes; more moochers; relatives; etc. It was an all-you-can-eat buffet at the bank. An army of termites munched through 10 million rupees ($222,000) in currency notes stored in a steel chest at a bank in northern India. The bank manager discovered the damage when he opened the reinforced room in an old bank building. If you become wealthy, human termites will show up on your doorstep. Bill Curry of south Boston worked most of his life as a cafeteria cook for the Merit Food Company— modest income but he managed to provide for his wife and his son and his daughter. So when Bill Curry won the state lottery, 3.6 million dollars, his first thought was just to buy a Dalmatian puppy for the youngsters. That was the extent of the celebration. But then the parasites converged—the lawyers and the investment advisers, the accountants and the financial analysts—he was overwhelmed by them. And by people wanting handouts for all manner of charities. He returned to his job in the cafeteria, but even there financial advisers were everywhere. His nearest relative says there's no doubt about it, in the weeks since he won the lottery, it was not the money that caused his stress but it was all of those people who wanted to deal themselves in. Bill Curry has died of a heart attack at 37.

WEALTH DOES NOT MAKE ONE *SLEEPY*

[13]*The sleep of a laboring man is sweet, Whether he eats little or much; But the abundance of the rich will not permit him to sleep* – Why? He tosses and turns all night worrying about the stock market; his competitors; that someone will steal something from him or take advantage of him.

WEALTH DOES NOT GIVE ONE *SECURITY*

The world's Principle: Get to keep! [13] There is a severe evil *which* I have seen under the sun: Riches kept for their owner to his hurt – that principle is not from God (2 Cor. 9:6-11/Lu. 16:9-13). Some things are not meant to be kept! Imagine seeing an eagle in a field. You hurry to build a high fence around it. But that eagle simply spreads its wings and off it goes! An eagle cannot be kept in a fence! Money is like that – it has wings! When it is used as a means of ministering, it is as beautiful as that eagle. But if we try to keep money, it will take wings and fly away!

Wealth is an Uncertainty

Therefore the world has Trouble, because wealth has an air of *Uncertainty* about it. *[14] But those riches perish through misfortune; When he begets a son, there is nothing in his hand-* as I have often said, "There is always something!" Some expense, some misfortune that drains the wallet! Stock markets crash and nest eggs suddenly fall out of trees.

Wealth cannot help when one enters *Eternity*.

[15] As he came from his mother's womb, naked shall he return, To go as he came; And he shall take nothing from his labor Which he may carry away in his hand. [16] And this also is a severe evil-- Just exactly as he came, so shall he go. And what profit has he who has labored for the wind? [17] All his days he also eats in darkness, And he has much sorrow and sickness and anger.

Death separates everyone from their money! Cecil Rhodes spent years exploiting the natural resources of South Africa. When he was about to die, he cried out in remorse: "I've found much in Africa. Diamonds, gold and land are mine, but now I must leave them all behind. Not a thing I've gained can be taken with me. I have not sought eternal treasures; therefore I actually have nothing at all."

But there is also a wealth that is *Undeniable*.

[18] Here is what I have seen: It is good and fitting for one to eat and drink, and to enjoy the good of all his labor in which he toils under the sun all the days of his life which God gives him; for it is his heritage. [19] As for every man to whom God has given riches and wealth, and given him power to eat of it, to receive his heritage and rejoice in his

labor--this is the gift of God. [20] *For he will not dwell unduly on the days of his life, because God keeps him busy with the joy of his heart*

One noted, "Refuse to allow yourself to get caught in the greed trap. Refuse to attach yourself to the dollar sign. Refuse to place top priority on making more – just to make more! It's not always true that there's a better joy around the corner. The greener grass is indeed a myth. So find fulfillment in your work. Invest more in the vertical dimensions of life, less in the horizontal. Invest our riches for God's work. Invest time for His glory. Give generously. That way you'll find a rejoicing in your labor that gives a new dimension."

WEALTHY DOES NOT GIVE *SERENITY.*
The *Lamenting* of treasure without pleasure.

The *Good* things brought no pleasure. He has a full *Liter* but no pleasure. *If a man begets a hundred children...* - children are a treasure but often bring more grief then pleasure. They are clearly no substitute for God!

He had *Longevity* but not pleasure *and lives many years, so that the days of his years are many, but his soul is not satisfied with goodness...* – old age is viewed as a treasure but again a long life does not necessarily bring pleasure. Read ahead to Eccles. 12! He has fruitful *Labors* but no pleasure in them. *All the labor of man is for his mouth, And yet the soul is not satisfied* – working keeps food on the table but not satisfaction in the soul. He has *Learning* but not pleasure from his learning. [8] *For what more has the wise man than the fool? What does the poor man have, Who knows how to walk before the living?* [9] *Better is the sight of the eyes than the wandering of desire. This also is vanity and grasping for the wind* - education is not all it's cracked up to be! Good things like – children; old age; a good job; and a good education; are not the source of our serenity and joy.

Swindoll, "He begins by adding many children. Maybe having more children will make life more satisfying. But having many children won't make a depressed life free from depression. Well, some would say we need to add more years. Maybe what is needed is a longer life. If your life is marked by pain and hardship and emptiness, what good is it to add to it a thousand years? That only adds a thousand more sorrows. Well, maybe what we need is to add work. But work doesn't bring satisfaction to an empty life. Since no one of those things help, maybe we should add a bright mind, wisdom, a good education? Solomon seems to shout at the himself – "Stop dreaming! Stop thinking you can add a few details that will make you think you can put color into a life that is grim. Many children? Who are you kidding! Many wives? More years? Longer hours? Better education? Brighter mind? No, a thousand times no – it won't work! Come to terms with reality. Face the inescapable truth – *You Need God!*"

Notice the *Grave* brought shame...*or indeed he has no burial* – the idea is that even with all of his children, grey hairs, successful job, and degrees he is still not given a proper burial! Which in that culture is a disgrace. Jer. 8:2; 14:16; 16:4,6; 25:33 He is Lamenting these treasures because they bring him no real serenity.

The *Likening* of treasure without pleasure to a *Miscarriage*.

- He says both are *Useless...I say that a stillborn child is better than he- for it comes in vanity...* - the idea is that just as it seems useless for a baby to be conceived just to die; so it seems useless to live and yet find no pleasure out of life.

- Both are *Unimportant, and departs in darkness, and its name is covered with darkness* – the stillborn baby is taken from the womb to the grave. Thus the baby makes no impact on society, has no accomplishments or achievements; just like the person who lives under the sun.

- Both are Unsatisfied. *⁵ Though it has not seen the sun or known anything, this has more rest than that man, ⁶ even if he lives a thousand years twice--but has not seen goodness...* – the baby never sees the sun, never enjoys life; just as the one living under the sun.

- Both are *Uprooted...Do not all go to one place? ⁷ All the labor of man is for his mouth, And yet the soul is not satisfied. ⁸ For what more has the wise man than the fool? What does the poor man have, Who knows how to walk before the living? ⁹ Better is the sight of the eyes than the wandering of desire. This also is vanity and grasping for the wind* – the point is both the stillborn and the unsatisfied end up dead! The stillborn is likened to the Unsatisfied!

"³...I'd say that a stillborn baby gets the better deal. ⁴ It gets its start in a mist and ends up in the dark—unnamed. ⁵ It sees nothing and knows nothing, but is better off by far than anyone living. ⁶ Even if someone lived a thousand years— make it two thousand!—but didn't enjoy anything, what's the point? Doesn't everyone end up in the same place? ⁷ We work to feed our appetites; Meanwhile our souls go hungry. ⁸ So what advantage has a sage over a fool, or over some poor wretch who barely gets by? ⁹ Just grab whatever you can while you can; don't assume something better might turn up by and by. All it amounts to anyway is smoke. And spitting into the wind." Ecclesiastes 6:3-9 (MSG)

Anderson, "From the sinkhole of depression can spew forth some of the most senseless, angry words. Depression speaks a totally foreign language at times. As it gropes for meaning, it looks at anything and everything that might be its cause and sometimes draws some very foolish conclusions. Much of what Solomon spouts in Ecclesiastes has its roots in the fact that he is severely depressed." But why is he depressed? We would say he has forgotten to take his medicine and failure to surround himself with people who will pander to his self-pity. But in reality he is depressed because he has forgotten God!

Treasure without pleasure causes one to be guilty of *Lambasting* God.

  ❋ Our Fate is Fixed

¹⁰ *Whatever one is, he has been named already-* "¹⁰ Whatever happens, happens. Its destiny is fixed. You can't argue with fate." Ecclesiastes 6:10 (MSG)

"Fate, personified by the Greeks under the name of Moira, signified in the ancient world the unseen power that rules over human destiny. In classical thought fate was believed to be superior to the gods, since even they were unable to defy its all-encompassing power. Fate is not chance, which may be defined as the absence of laws, but instead a cosmic determinism that has no ultimate meaning or purpose. In classical thought as well as in Oriental religion, fate is a dark, sinister power related to the tragic vision of life. It connotes not the absence of freedom but the subjection of freedom. It is the transcendent necessity in which freedom is entangled (Tillich). Fate is blind, inscrutable, and inescapable. Christianity substituted for the Hellenistic concept of fate the doctrine of divine providence. Whereas fate is the portentous, impersonal power that thwarts and overrules human freedom, providence liberates people to fulfill the destiny for which they were created. Fate means the abrogation of freedom; providence means the realization of authentic freedom through submission to divine guidance. Providence is the direction and support of a loving God, which makes life ultimately bearable; fate is the rule of contingency that casts a pall over all human striving. Whereas fate makes the future precarious and uncertain, providence fills the future with hope. Fate is impersonal and irrational; providence is supremely personal and [supernaturally rational]." [Evangelical Dictionary of Theology]

* Our efforts are *Feeble. For it is known that he is man; And he cannot contend with Him who is mightier than he-* fatalism views an impersonal force behind everything, but because Solomon is a true believer he inconsistently combines fatalism with providence.

The point is this – God will not let one enjoy treasure with pleasure when He is left out of the picture. No one can successfully prevail over God.

* Our words are *Futile.* Since there are many things that increase vanity, How *is* man the better? – many things = many words.

For there are many words which increase futility. What *then* is the advantage to a man? Ecclesiastes 6:11

* Our life is *Fleeting. For who knows what is good for man in life, all the days of his vain life which he passes like a shadow?* Our *Future* is *Foggy...Who can tell a man what will happen after him under the sun?* Solomon is not right with God, if he was, he would focus on eternal treasures which alone bring present pleasures. The vanity of trying to find satisfaction in wealth. I think Dobson summed it up well:

"I have concluded that accumulation of wealth, even if I could achieve it, is an insufficient reason for living. When I reach the end of my days, a moment or two from now, I must look backward on something more meaningful than the pursuit of houses and land and machines and stocks and bonds. Nor is fame of any lasting benefit. I will consider my earthly existence to have been wasted unless I can recall an earnest attempt to serve the God who made me. Nothing else makes sense, and certainly nothing else is worthy of my agitation."

CHAPTER 11

Words

§

(Wise sayings)

Talk in everlasting words
And dedicate them all to me
I will give you all my life
It's here if you should call to me

You think that I don't even mean
A single word I say
It's only words and words are all I have
To take your heart away

[Recorded: 1969-08-25, first released on In Person]

WHEN I WAS LOST I heard a saying that went something like this, "Look for something in another life, but don't be too set on what it is, that way you will not be disappointed." I remember taking a lot of comfort from that wise quote, but it proved to be an inadequate saying to live by, time and time again. The Vanity of life is seen in the inadequacy of Wise sayings.

Swindoll, "We have reached the halfway point in Solomon's journal. The man is describing life under the sun – ragged-edged reality without God. Thus far in his journal, that has been his mindset, and it continues to be but instead of continuing the narrative style he has employed so far, he turns to the proverbial style - brief, crisp, simple-sounding statements that offer insightful principle for handling life."

WISE SAYINGS RELATED TO THE BETTER THINGS OF LIFE. 7:1-12
REPUTATION IS BETTER THAN PERFUME

A Comparison. *A good name is better than precious ointment...* - a good reputation can have its advantages. Bill Gaither wanted to buy a piece of land where he could build. He found the property he wanted. The owner, a 92 year old retired banker, Mr. Yule. Mr. Yule refused to sell the land because he had promised the neighboring farmers could use it for their cattle. He asked Bill what his name was and Bill said, "Bill Gaither." The owner asked, "Are you any relation to Grover Gaither?" Bill replied, "Yes, he was my grandfather." Mr. Yule said, "Grover Gaither was the best worker I ever had on my farm. Full day's work for a day's pay. So honest. What did you say you wanted?" Because of Bill's Grandfathers reputation the old man sold Bill the property. And yet, it is not always possible to have a good reputation when you live for Jesus Christ.

* William Booth founder of the Salvation Army was often ridiculed and attacked for his faith in Christ.
* D. L. Moody was nicknamed "Crazy Moody."
* It was said of Spurgeon, "They said he was preaching an outmoded gospel, pure foolishness. The sophisticated commentators of his day argued that his popularity with the rabble would be short lived. He would be up like a rocket and down like a stick!" Spurgeon himself once said, "If I lost my reputation, I wouldn't walk across the street to pick it up!"

Woe to you when all men speak well of you, For so did their fathers to the false prophets. Luke 6:26

It's better than *precious ointment* – lit. "then olive oil." Actually olive oil was very useful, it was used for cooking (1 Ki. 17:12-16); in the offering unto God (Lev. 2:15-16); for anointing Prophets (Isa. 61:), Priests (Lev. 8:30), and Kings

(1 Sam. 10:1; 16:13); for Healing (Isa.1:6); for lighting (Ex. 25:6; 27:20); for attracting (Song of Sol. 1:3; 4:10); and as a perfume. His point is that Perfume gives off a pleasant and noticeable aroma but is short lived while a reputation is pleasant and noticeable but lasts a long time…But when you face a storm in your life, neither a good reputation nor expensive perfume will be of much good. Truth is our name is Christian – who has ever really lived up to that name? Swedish tax authorities refused a request by Sara Leisten to name her newborn son after the superhero. The officials were following legislation giving them veto power over names. They rejected Sara's request citing its potential to attract ridicule later in life. Sara plans to re-apply, one thing is clear, little Superman would have a name he can never live up to.

A FUNERAL IS BETTER THAN A FESTIVAL
…And the day of death than the day of one's birth [2] *Better to go to the house of mourning Than to go to the house of feasting, For that is the end of all men; And the living will take it to heart.* [3] *Sorrow is better than laughter, For by a sad countenance the heart is made better.* [4] *The heart of the wise is in the house of mourning, But the heart of fools is in the house of mirth* – our death day is better than our birthday.

There is Relief and meaningful Reflection in death. Yet man is born to trouble, As the sparks fly upward. Job 5:7. Keep in mind one living under the sun believes neither in heaven or hell. All he knows is that life is full of pain and misery – and as far as he can see that all ends at the grave. There is no Real lasting benefit from a festival. Swindoll, "Visiting a funeral parlor is better than gorging oneself at a banquet or a thirty-minute stroll through a graveyard is better than an entire afternoon at a carnival or spending a weekend in Vegas."

CORRECTION IS BETTER THAN CONGRATULATION
[5] *It is better to hear the rebuke of the wise Than for a man to hear the song of fools.*

[6] *For like the crackling of thorns under a pot, So is the laughter of the fool. This also is vanity* – we would rather be congratulated but we learn more from a rebuke. But again outward correction cannot transform the heart. In a movie Wild in

the Country, Glen corrects a loose woman, "Get your mind out of the gutter!" She says, "It doesn't do no good, it just goes right back down again."

JUSTICE IS BETTER THAN INJUSTICE
⁷ Surely oppression destroys a wise man's reason, And a bribe debases the heart — that's true, but knowing that doesn't produce justice. Truth is God allows oppression regardless of our opposition to it. One man said to a friend, "Sometimes I would like to ask God why He allows poverty, famine, and injustice when He could do something about it." His friend replied, "Well, then why don't you?" He said, "Because I'm afraid He might ask me the same question!"

PATIENCE IS BETTER THAN PRIDE
⁸ The end of a thing is better than its beginning; The patient in spirit is better than the proud in spirit. ⁹ Do not hasten in your spirit to be angry, For anger rests in the bosom of fools — we all need to push aside our pride and be patient with one another. We can write that on our refrigerator door and memorize it but if we leave God out of the picture we will soon find that impatience and pride are both our constant companions! Many people living under the sun have wise and noble sayings but such sayings will not satisfy because we cannot practice them. Often we replace God's Law with our sayings but the end result is the same!

¹⁴ For what I am doing, I do not understand. ¹⁵For what I will to do, that I do not practice; but what I hate, that I do. ¹⁶ If, then, I do what I will not to do, I agree with the law that *it is* good. ¹⁷ But now, *it is* no longer I who do it, but sin that dwells in me. ¹⁸ For I know that in me (that is, in my flesh) nothing good dwells; for to will is present with me, but *how* to perform what is good I do not find. ¹⁹ For the good that I will *to do,* I do not do; but the evil I will not *to do,* that I practice. ²⁰ Now if I do what I will not *to do,* it is no longer I who do it, but sin that dwells in me. ²¹ I find then a law, that evil is present with me, the one who wills to do good. ²² For I delight in the law of God according to the inward man.

[23] But I see another law in my members, warring against the law of my mind, and bringing me into captivity to the law of sin which is in my members. Romans 7:15-23

The sin nature cannot be potty trained – not even with wise saying words. Near Watsonville, California, there is a creek that has a strange name: Salsipuedes Creek. *Salsi puedes* is Spanish for *"Get out of it, if you can."* The creek is lined with quicksand, and the story is that many years ago, in the early days of California, a Mexican laborer fell into the quicksand. A Spaniard, riding by on a horse, saw him and yelled out to him, *"Salsi puedes!"* The creek has been so named ever since. That is what the flesh is like. We struggle to correct these tendencies, to get out of the effects of our sinful nature, but we cannot do it in our own strength, not even armed with cute wise sayings. It's only by God's Spirit (Gal. 5:16).

WISE SAYINGS RELATED TO THE BITTER THINGS IN LIFE

LIFE IS *UNCHANGEABLE*

[13] Consider the work of God; For who can make straight what He has made crooked? [14] In the day of prosperity be joyful, But in the day of adversity consider: Surely God has appointed the one as well as the other, So that man can find out nothing *that will come* after him – again this is a wise saying, and at least he comes up again for a gulp of air, but knowing this does not solve all of our problems! It's bitter for people who want to control life to realize we are not in control. We all love to watch movies where the bad guy loses and the good guy is in control and takes charge. I call it the John Wayne mentality. In one movie, Cahill – US Marshall. It opens with John Wayne coming upon five heavily armed outlaws. He says: "Boys, I hear you robbed the bank. I'm here to bring you in. Are you ready to surrender?" They all start laughing. One of them says, "Surrender! There are five of us and only one of you." John Wayne says, "Yep, that's about the size of it. So does that mean you're gonna surrender or not?" One of them reaches for his gun and the bullets start flying. The next scene John Wayne is ridding off with the bad guys behind him most draped over their horses. But we all know, that in the real world, it would be John Wayne draped over his horse…Truth is we don't control the bad guys or much else

for that matter! Those living only under the sun are living in a fantasy, world cherishing their supposed freedom to control their lives. Freedom can become one's own god.

- Karl Marx: "Man is free only if he owes his existence to himself." (*19th century, Germany*)
- Friedrich Nietzsche: "If there were gods, who could bear not to be gods? Therefore there are no gods." (*19th century, Germany*)
- John F. Kennedy: "Man can be as big as he wants. No problem of human destiny is beyond human beings."

Life is Unreasonable

An Observation. *[15] I have seen everything in my days of vanity: There is a just man who perishes in his righteousness, And there is a wicked man who prolongs life in his wickedness* – he sees righteous people dying prematurely and wicked people living prolonged lives. We read about young godly men and women being killed on the mission field – and then we read about people like Hugh Hefner who this April turned 87 years old.

An Exhortation. Don't be excessively righteous and wise! *Do not be overly righteous, Nor be overly wise: Why should you destroy yourself?* – can one really be too righteous or wise? No, not if it's righteousness and wisdom from God. "Excessively [overly] refers to the tendency to self-righteousness. Solomon calls the reader to turn away from that kind of pretense. He says in effect, "Don't think of yourself as so righteous." Or "Do not pretend to be wise" or "Don't try to make yourself appear wise when you aren't." [A Handbook of Eccles.]

Often those who spout out all of these wise sayings are wise only in their own eyes...On the other hand, don't be excessively wicked. *Do not be overly wicked, Nor be foolish: Why should you die before your time?* – obviously living a reckless sinful life is flirting with danger. The Solution? It is good that you grasp this, And also not remove your hand from the other; For he who fears God will escape them all *[19] Wisdom strengthens the wise More than ten rulers of the city* – fearing God destroys self-righteousness and discourages sin. The problem is those living only under the sun have no regard for God.

[18] *"There is no fear of God before their eyes."* Romans 3:18

The Question comes that comes to mind is, why is life so unreasonable? It is because people are Unrighteous. *For there is not a just man on earth who does good And does not sin* – it only looks like there are righteous and unrighteous people. In reality there are no righteous people under the sun! It is also because sinful people are Unkind. Also do not take to heart everything people say, Lest you hear your servant cursing you. [22] For many times, also, your own heart has known That even you have cursed others – we are all unkind because we are all sinners – no exceptions! Spurgeon, "We will find that even those who live with us are not always singing our praises. Who has not, under temporary irritation said that of another, that which we have afterwards regretted. Would we not all be in an awkward position if we were called to account for every word we have spoken?" We could add in spite of our wise sayings, people are Unwise.

[23] *All this I have proved by wisdom. I said, "I will be wise"; But it was far from me.* [24] *As for that which is far off and exceedingly deep,*

Who can find it out? [25] *I applied my heart to know, To search and seek out wisdom and the reason of things, To know the wickedness of folly, Even of foolishness and madness.* [26] *And I find more bitter than death The woman whose heart is snares and nets, Whose hands are fetters. He who pleases God shall escape from her, But the sinner shall be trapped by her.* [27] *"Here is what I have found," says the Preacher, "Adding one thing to the other to find out the reason,* [28] *Which my soul still seeks but I cannot find: One man among a thousand I have found, But a woman among all these I have not found.* [29] *Truly, this only I have found: That God made man upright, But they have sought out many schemes."* – is it not bitter to know that the problem with the world is found within each one of us!

Swindoll, "Our basic problems are not above us; they are within us. They are not around us; they are within us. They're not with God; they are with ourselves. The very ones God made upright have sought out many many devices. We have become creative, but our creativity is misdirected and our devices are destructive. We have replaced genuine righteousness with a mask of righteousness. And none of our man devices brings us back to God. On the contrary they push us further away from him."

The Vanity of life is seen in the inadequacy of Wise sayings. In self-righteousness many hide behind a barrage of wise saying, but as reality sets in, we realize these sayings do not bring satisfaction or solutions to our problems. It didn't take me long to realize that my wise saying, "Look for something in another life, but don't be too set on what it is, that way you will not be disappointed" wasn't going to get me through life!

CHAPTER 12

Tell me Why

§

(Not knowing the Why's of life)

Every time I look at someone new
Tell me why I think of you
Then you sometimes ask me by
You're playing with love
Darling tell me why

You left me all alone
To cry over you
My heart is torn and broken
There's nothing left to do

In my prayers, I'll mention you
When you're gone I feel so blue
Why can't I have all of you
Oh, somebody, please tell me why

[Recorded: 1957/01/12, first released on single]

A 2011 article in *National Geographic* asks:

"MOODY. IMPULSIVE. MADDENING. WHY DO teenagers act the way they do?" The
article implies that gaining insight into the huge changes in a teenager's brain could

help parents understand their children's unpredictable moods and behaviors. It also shows why parents need to provide firm but loving guidance during this critical phase of development. The article states: The first series of scans of the developing brain ... showed that our brains undergo a massive reorganization between our 12th and 25th year. The brain doesn't actually grow much during this period .... But as we move through adolescence, the brain undergoes extensive remodeling, resembling a network and wiring upgrade. When this "upgrade" to the brain is finally complete, the entire brain will work much faster. It will also enable young adults to balance impulse, risk, desire, and personal goals. But the article warns:

But at times, especially at first, the brain does this work clumsily. It's hard to get all those new cogs to mesh .... These studies also explain why teens behave with such vexing inconsistency: beguiling at breakfast, disgusting at dinner; masterful on Monday, sleepwalking on Saturday. Along with lacking experience generally, they're still learning to use their brain's new network. Stress, fatigue, or challenges can cause a misfire. [A psychologist who studies teens] calls this neural gawkiness—an equivalent to the physical awkwardness teens sometimes display while mastering their growing bodies.

The article reveals our desire to know the Why's of life. But I assure you everything in that article will be brought into question several years from now. Truth is we usually do not know the Why's of life. The vanity comes from not knowing the Why's of life.

WHY IS LIFE LIKE THIS? 8:1-17

The effect that wisdom has on a *Person,* we begin with the Question. *Who is like the wise man and who knows the interpretation of a matter? –* who can really interpret what life is all about? Nobody! Only God can interpret life...

[8] Then they said to him, "We have had a dream and there is no one to interpret it." Then Joseph said to them, "Do not interpretations belong to God? Tell *it* to me, please." Genesis 40:8

[27] Daniel answered before the king and said, "As for the mystery about which the king has inquired, neither wise men, conjurers, magicians *nor* diviners are able to declare *it* to the king. [28] "However, there is a God in heaven who reveals mysteries Daniel 2:27-28

An Observation. *A man's wisdom illumines him and causes his stern face to beam –* wisdom is reflected in his face. An adviser to Lincoln recommended a particular person for a cabinet position, but Lincoln balked at the suggestion. He said "I don't like the man's face." "But, sir." said the adviser, "he can't be held responsible for his face." Lincoln replied, "Every man over forty is responsible for his face." Human wisdom may cause one to have a friendly face, but he still does not know how to interpret the meaning of life apart from God. We see the king's *Punishment.* We are introduced to one who renders Obedience to the king. *I say, "Keep the command of the king –* Solomon's power was absolute. It could do as he pleased without any Congress or Supreme Court to stay his hand. It was foolish not to obey him. The Oath that should be remembered. He says, *because of the oath before God -* people work in the king's palace, they will do what the king says, partly because they have sworn before God to be obedient. There should be an obliging attitude. *³"Do not be in a hurry to leave him. Do not join in an evil matter, for he will do whatever he pleases."⁴ Since the word of the king is authoritative, who will say to him, "What are you doing?" –* to disrespect or take part in a conspiracy against the king is extremely dangerous. The Outcome of such a fine citizen? Here is where the mystery comes in; you would think things would go well for such a model citizen…At first, there is Protection from harm. *He who keeps a royal command experiences no trouble,* because he knows and follows proper Procedures. It notes, *for a wise heart knows the proper time and procedure for every delight –* he knows When and How to speak. But he quickly adds a note of perplexity, *though a man's trouble is heavy upon him –* in spite of being careful not to offend the king he ends up in trouble. Why is this? Who knows but it happens! Even a wise man does not know the Future. *If no one knows what will happen, who can tell him when it will happen?*

"⁷ Since no man knows the future, who can tell him what is to come?" Ecclesiastes 8:7

Even a wise man will have a Fatality. *No man has authority to restrain the wind with the wind, or authority over the day of death; and there is no discharge in the time of war, and evil will not deliver those [from death] who practice it –* again death comes to all and no one knows when. We cannot be released from death any more than a soldier who is in the midst of a battle can get permission to go home. And when all is said and done power always ends up abusing someone. *All this I have seen* and applied my mind to every deed that has been done under the sun wherein a man has exercised authority over another man to his hurt.

⁹ All this I observed as I tried my best to understand all that's going on in this world. As long as men and women have the power to hurt each other, this is the way it is. Ecclesiastes 8:9 (MSG)

Why does a wise Person ended up being Punished by the Government? Who knows? I think of David who could have taken King Saul's life and yet refused – the result of David's loyalty and respect? Saul sought to kill David for years. And then the evil man is Praised! The People who praise the wicked are identified, *So then, I have seen the wicked buried, those who used to go in and out from the holy place, and they are soon forgotten [praised] in the city where they did thus. This too is futility* – by the very people who had experienced the evil! The NIV follows certain manuscripts as well as the LXX. The Hebrew text seems to have a verb which means "to forget." A better translation is: "Then I saw that wicked people were given a public burial. They were taken from the holy place and buried; and they were praised by the people in the city – the very place where they committed their evil acts. How could this happen?" Actually this is common – I have been to funerals where what was said about the person caused me to wonder if they buried the wrong person! Why is it even the most wicked sinner tends to be spoken well of when he dies? I don't know! To make things worse the Punishment of the wicked is Postponed. Because the sentence against an evil deed is not executed quickly, therefore the hearts of the sons of men among them are given fully to do evil – those terrorists who killed four American's in the Benghazi attack still have not been brought to justice. And that was back on September 11th, 2012! Oddly enough the wicked person's life may be Prolonged.

Although a sinner does evil a hundred times and may lengthen his life, still I know that it will be well for those who fear God, who fear Him openly ¹³ *But it will not be well for the evil man and he will not lengthen his days like a shadow, because he does not fear God.* – it is better to fear God, but we cannot help but wonder why the sinner who does evil 100 times lives so long? But they do die soon enough and even the longest of lives seems like a passing shadow – they go by quickly. There is no hard and fast rule – the wicked may live a long life or they may die young.

[15] Even though a person sins and gets by with it hundreds of times throughout a long life, I'm still convinced that the good life is reserved for the person who fears God, who lives reverently in his presence, [13] and that the evil person will not experience a "good" life. No matter how many days he lives, they'll all be as flat and colorless as a shadow— because he doesn't fear God. Ecclesiastes 8:12-13 (MSG)

If at times what Solomon says is confusing and even contradictory – that is to be expected when life is viewed from merely an earthly perspective. Point is often the wicked do not get what they deserve - a short painful life, exposed for the sinners they are… Followed on the heels of all this is the Why's related to the evil mans Prosperity. There is the reaping; there is futility which is done on the earth, that is, there are righteous men to whom it happens according to the deeds of the wicked. On the other hand, there are evil men to whom it happens according to the deeds of the righteous. I say that this too is futility – it looks like the righteous reap, what the wicked sow; and the wicked seem to reap, what the righteous sow! You can only accept Gal. 6:7 by faith…The Response? So I commended pleasure, for there is nothing good for a man under the sun except to eat and to drink and to be merry, and this will stand by him in his toils *throughout* the days of his life which God has given him under the sun. Swindoll, "In a world of unjust triumph and unfair consequences, I see an individual here who is a personification of the mystery of untimely pleasure. [How should we respond? Fear and enjoy God]. What's the alternative? The alternative is to become bitter, cynical, questioning, never at peace, neurotic in one's pursuit of answers to why, why, why! Instead of going mad, attempting to solve all the mysteries of heaven and earth, which cannot be done, the writer suggests a simple plan: Eat, Drink, and happily trust God!"

It is the Lord's Privilege alone to know the whys!

[16] *When I gave my heart to know wisdom and to see the task which has been done on the earth (even though one should never sleep day or night),* [17] *and I saw every work of God, I concluded that man cannot discover the work which has been done under the sun. Even though man should seek laboriously, he will not discover; and though the wise man should say, "I know," he cannot discover* - Dt. 29:29

Don Anderson, "Let's therefore not agonize over the perplexities and seeming injustices of life. God is in charge. He is in control. Our job is to enjoy the existence He has given us, trusting in Him, hoping in Him – and not worrying about what we cannot understand or change." There is a TV show called "Unsolved Mysteries." You can watch week after week life's unsolved mysteries – they never run out of material because life is filled with unanswered Why's!

WHY'S RELATED TO THE LOSS OF LIFE 9:1-12

* Loss of life does not allow God to be Understandable.

Note: The "when" and "how" people die, causes many to assume God's favor or disfavor toward someone. If somebody lives to be an old age we assume they are blessed by God; and when someone dies young or in a violent fashion that it is related to judgment. God is in Control. *For I have taken all this to my heart and explain it that righteous men, wise men, and their deeds are in the hand of God.* God's Approval or Disapproval cannot be determined by life's Circumstances. *Man does not know whether it will be love or hatred; anything awaits him* – we do not know God's thoughts based on circumstances. "Because love and hate appear here without pronoun suffixes, Solomon is taking about God's love and hate rather than peoples. The entire verse can be rendered: "Now I studied all this and decided that God is in control of righteous and wise people and everything they do. They do not know whether God will accept or reject them. All of that lies in the future." [Handbook to Ecclessiates]

Leupold, "A man cannot tell whether God's attitude toward him is one of love or hatred. Everything is still before them. This means that practically anything can happen to a man. The "love" and the "hatred" referred to, must be thought of as attitudes of God, for God was just mentioned as having all issues in His hand, and the words that follow suggest that He may send anything. No man has a certainty as to the next thing that shall befall him."

But whatever comes our way it is no indication of what God thinks of us. Gibson, "It is of great importance for our peace of mind to firmly grasp the thought that we cannot at all infer what God thinks or intends concerning any person or his works from outward circumstances we observe." We might look at Abrahams life and concluded that God loved him because he made him prosperous (Gen. 13:2) but ungodly Haman was also outwardly prosperous (Est. 5:11); One might conclude that wicked Ahab was judged for his wickedness because he was killed in battle (1 Ki.22:34) but the problem is that godly Josiah was also killed in battle (2 Ki. 23:29).

[1] Now on the same occasion there were some present who reported to Him about the Galileans whose blood Pilate had mixed with their sacrifices. [2] And Jesus said to them, "Do you suppose that these Galileans were *greater* sinners than all *other* Galileans because they suffered this *fate?* [3] "I tell you, no, but unless you repent, you will all likewise perish. [4] "Or do you suppose that those eighteen on whom the tower in Siloam fell and killed them were *worse* culprits than all the men who live in Jerusalem? [5] "I tell you, no, but unless you repent, you will all likewise perish."

Luke 13:1-5

Then how do we know what God thinks of a person? Only by God's inspired Word. It is clear that there are only two kinds of people – those In Adam and those In Christ. The first is under God's wrath and the latter are blessed with all spiritual blessings in heavenly places in Christ (Eph.1:3).

* Loss of life is also Inescapable

It is the same for all. There is one fate for the righteous and for the wicked; for the good, for the clean and for the unclean; for the man who offers a sacrifice and for the one who does not sacrifice. As the good man is, so is the sinner; as the swearer is, so is the one who is afraid to swear [to take an oath carelessly [3] *This is an evil in all that is done under the sun, that there is one fate for all men. Furthermore, the hearts of the sons of men are full of evil and insanity is in their hearts throughout their lives. Afterwards they go to the dead* – under the sun people are divided into good and bad based upon what they do. But God says there are none who do good (Rom. 3:11) and thus all die (Rom.6:23). But if you leave God's Word out, then you cannot help but wonder why the good should die like the bad?

 ❦   Loss of life is also Undesirable
    Death brings loss of Confidence.

For whoever is joined with all the living, there is hope; surely a live dog is better than a dead lion – dogs in that day were dangerous, starving scavengers. But it is better to be a living mangy mutt then a dead majestic lion! The word "hope" is a rare Hebrew word found only here and in 2 Ki. 18:19 and Isa. 36:4. The root word means "to have confidence." And yet the confidence of the living is ruined by thought of the certainty of death. Earnest Hemingway, "Life is a dirty trick, a short journey from nothingness to nothingness. There is no remedy for anything in life. Man's destiny in the universe is like a colony of ants on a burning log."

Death brings loss of Consciousness.

For the living know they will die; but the dead do not know anything. . . – many people believe that death just ends it all.

Death brings a loss of Compensation

. . .nor have they any longer a reward, for their memory is forgotten – the idea is that when you die there are no more paychecks!

Death brings a loss of Contribution

Indeed their love, their hate and their zeal have already perished, and they will no longer have a share in all that is done under the sun – Johnny Carson, "For three days after death, hair and fingernails continue to grow, but phone calls taper off!" He fires off one thought after another:

 ❦   Loss of life is Unacceptable. 7-10

Note: Keep in mind the context – he is not saying the following is good. He is just presenting how people cope with death who are confined to life under the sun. They basically try to ignore it.

Live life to the Fullest. 7-8

Let's live for our Families. 9

Let's live to be Fruitful. 10

The idea is do anything you can to keep your mind off death. But even with all the distractions we cannot help be confronted with death – those gray hairs; those funerals we have to attend; those birthdays; etc. Billy Crystal in City Slickers turns to his boss and says, "Have you ever reached a point in your life where you say to yourself, 'This is the best I'm ever gonna look, this is the best I'm ever gonna feel, this is the best I'm ever gonna do – and it ain't that great!"

* Loss of life is Unpredictable. 11-12

The Events in Life. 11

<u>I again saw under the sun that the race is not to the swift and the battle is not to the warriors, and neither is bread to the wise nor wealth to the discerning nor favor to men of ability; for time and chance overtake them all</u> – why is not the race to the swift? Or the battle to the warriors? Because of something that stops all events of life – death!

The End of life. 12

The End is Unknown, *Moreover, man does not know his time:* - we know we're going to die, but we have no idea when. The End is also Unexpected, like fish caught in a treacherous net and birds trapped in a snare, so the sons of men are ensnared at an evil time when it suddenly falls on them – even though we know we're going to die, it is a surprise when it happens.

WHY IS THEIR A LACK OF APPRECIATION FOR THE LEARNED 9:13-18

Wisdom often goes Unrewarded. Again we must keep ever before us Solomon's *Perspective. Also this I came to see as wisdom under the sun – we will never understand* this book unless we realize it is from an "under the sun" perspective. Solomon's Impression, *and it impressed me* – the idea is that it affected him profoundly. Solomon then gives a Parable.

* A City. *There was a small city with few men in it* – a small unimpressive place.
* A Crisis, *and a great king came to it, surrounded it and constructed large siege works against it* – a powerful king surrounded the city and prepared to attack it.
* A Champion - *But there was found in it a poor wise man and he delivered the city by his wisdom* – this poor wise man delivered the city by way of his wisdom.
* A Congratulations...not! *Yet no one remembered that poor man* – any thanks he received was short lived. Why? Wisdom goes unappreciated in this world...Reminds me of a retired couple. He decided that since he was now retired he should help with the chores. Both of them loved oatmeal for breakfast. He decided that he would take part in making the morning oatmeal. He got a notebook and pencil and asked his wife for insight into how to make oatmeal. She said: "Be sure to measure the water and the oats; use the small sauce pan; be sure to stir it carefully when cooling so that it doesn't stick; don't forget to time it; when it is fully cooked turn off the gas; put a lid on the pan and let it stand for a few minutes before serving; before you wash the saucepan, soak it in warm water for a while..." Later his wife glanced in his notebook, the first page read, "Forget the oatmeal!"

Furthermore wisdom is often Unappreciated. As stated wisdom is Invaluable, that poor wise man did save the city. Like the frail old man whose house kept getting pelted by kids throwing rocks at it. He offered to pay them $5 dollars for throwing rocks at his house and they gladly agreed. The next day he said, "Boys I can only afford to pay $1 for throwing the rocks." They were disappointed but agreed. The next day he offered them only 25 cents – and they said, "No way! Forget it! We are not going to throw rocks for only 5 cents." And they never threw rocks at his house again!

Wisdom is also Ignored. So I said, "Wisdom is better than strength." But the wisdom of the poor man is despised and his words are not heeded – this is why we are wise to live life with eternity in mind. Even though we speak wisdom when we share God's Word most people will not take the message to heart.

Our reward and appreciation comes from God and usually not until we enter eternity – and not from man. Last wisdom usually goes Unnoticed. The Contrast. *The words of the wise heard in quietness are better than the shouting of a ruler among fools* – even words whispered, so that you would have to strain to hear them, are better than the loud clear words of a fool. The Conclusion. *Wisdom is better than weapons of war, but one sinner destroys much good* – a fool destroys much good – why? Because people listen to them. But why? Who knows! I read about a school boy who was expelled from school for misbehaving. He stood outside and threw rocks against the window. The principle asked the boy what he was doing. He replied, "I just wanted everyone to know that I'm still here!"

A fool always carries plenty of rocks in their pocket, making sure everybody knows they're still around. The true wise do not have to be noticed by anyone but God.

Vanity comes from not knowing the Why's of life. Tullian Tchividjian tells the following story about trying to deal with the pain of his parent's unexpected divorce: I remember going to see [the Christian counselor] Larry Crabb, who was [a colleague of] my father.

"How's your mom and dad doing?" Larry asked. "Larry, I don't know what to do. Seriously, I feel like my whole world has been turned upside down. I don't get this. It's excruciating." Larry said something remarkable. He could see that I was trapped in the prison of Why, banging my head against the bars. He said, Tullian, listen to me: The "why" is none of your concern. This is not your burden to fix or figure out. You are not responsible for your parents' relationship or their reputation, or even your own reputation. Those are in God's hands, and his ways are His, not ours. When it comes to God's will, the sooner you can get out of the conjecture business, the better. *If you don't go to your grave confused, you don't go to your grave trusting.* Painful as it is, this situation gives you an opportunity to show them grace, to love them in their brokenness in a new way. Which is precisely what Jesus has done for you and continues to do for you. Larry preached the Gospel to me that day, and it made all the difference.

CHAPTER 13

Fool, Fool, Fool

§

(Putting up with the Nitwit's of life)

Fool, fool, fool
That I was to fall for you.
Well, fool, fool, fool
That I was to fall for you.
Well, I know what a fool I was
To think that you could love me, too.

Well, well, when I first met you, baby,
Well, I knew I couldn't win,
But I just kept right on trying,
'Cause trying is no sin.

What a fool, fool, fool,
That I was to fall for you.
Well, I know what a fool I was
To think that you could love me, too.

Well, when I first met you, baby,
Well, I knew I couldn't win,
But I just kept right on trying,
'Cause trying is no sin.

What a fool that I was to fall for you.
Well, I know what a fool I was
To think that you could love me too.

[Recorded: 1955/01 or 1955/02, first released on The King of Rock 'n' Roll]

I READ A TRUE STORY that took place out in San Francisco. A man, wanting to rob a downtown Bank of America, walked into the branch and wrote "This iz a stikkup. Put all your muny in this bag." While standing in line, waiting to give his note to the teller, he began to worry that someone had seen him write the note and might call the police before he reached the teller window. So he left the Bank of America and crossed the street to Wells Fargo. After waiting a few minutes in line, he handed his note to the Wells Fargo teller. She read it and, surmising from his spelling errors that he was not the brightest light in the harbor, she told him: "Sir, I cannot accept this note because it is written on a Bank of America deposit slip, you have to either fill out a Wells Fargo deposit slip or go back to Bank of America." The man said "OK" and left the Wells Fargo. The Wells Fargo teller then called the police who arrested the man a few minutes later, as he was waiting in line back at the Bank of America. Life has no shortage of fools, and part of the vanity of life is that we have to deal with them – and unfortunately we often encounter them in our own mirror! Vanity from having to put up with the Nitwit's of life. Let make sure we are on the same page, nit•wit ('nIt͵wIt) *n.* a slow-witted, stupid, or foolish person.

THE *CORRUPTION* THAT COMES FROM BEING A NITWIT. 10:1-7

A little folly can corrupt one's *Reputation*

He gives an Illustration. *Dead flies make a perfumer's oil stink, so a little foolishness is weightier than wisdom and honor.* [2] *A wise man's heart directs him toward the right, but the foolish man's heart directs him toward the left.* [3] *Even when the fool walks along the road, his sense is lacking and he demonstrates to everyone that he is a fool* – a tiny fly can ruin a large bottle of expensive perfume. The Application is obvious, in the same way a little foolishness can ruin one's reputation. Dog owner Peggy Ranger dropped off her six-year-old Shih Tzu, Stanley, at Montreal Dogs, a popular day care for dogs. Peggy only needed Stanley looked after for a few hours. Soon after dropping him off, Peggy got an urgent call from Montreal Dogs telling her that her dog had run away. For a full week the owners and employees at Montreal Dogs searched for

Stanley. So did Peggy's family and friends. They put up over 400 posters offering a $5,000 reward. They looked under cars, around dumpsters and the nearby railroad tracks. They put up notices online and in local newspapers. The owners phoned Peggy every day offering her encouragement and support. Peggy's sister told the media: "We went through hell, thinking somebody had kidnapped him, sold him to a pharmaceutical company, all the terrible things you think about when a dog is lost." After a week Peggy called a non-profit pet retrieval and rescue organization for help. Once they told the Montreal Dogs owners they would bring in a special tracking dog, and would be looking at the surveillance tapes from a business across the street that had the front entrance of Montreal Dogs in view, the owners finally confessed that they had lied about Stanley's "escape." In reality, Stanley had been mauled to death by at least four large dogs. The owners told reporters they had lied to spare Peggy Ranger the pain of knowing her dog had suffered such a horrific death. Peggy is suing the company. The owners of Montreal Dogs told the media, "In retrospect, it would have been best to tell the truth." A little foolishness caused Montreal Dogs to lose their reputation.

Then we see a little folly corrupts Rulers. A foolish ruler Abuses his Power. If the ruler's temper rises against you, do not abandon your position, because composure allays great offenses – don't panic if a ruler has a temper tantrum against you. Just calmly hold your ground until the anger subsides.

The fury of a king is *like* messengers of death
But a wise man will appease it. Proverbs16:14

A foolish rulers Position is Absurd

[5] There is an evil I have seen under the sun, like an error which goes forth from the ruler— [6] folly is set in many exalted places while rich men sit in humble places. [7] I have seen slaves *riding* on horses and princes walking like slaves on the land. Ecclesiastes 10:5-7

Most of us have seen the movie *The Sound of Music?* Liesl is the oldest girl in the Von Trapp family. A young Austrian named Rolf likes her. When we meet Rolf at the beginning of the movie, he is a submissive messenger boy. Then the Nazi's move into Austria and take over. Rolf becomes one of the Hitler youth and is given a whistle and a little authority. Suddenly, he has more power than Captain Von Trapp. When you're watching the movie, it is almost silly—this great and powerful man is being ordered around by this Nitwit boy! That's the way life often works – fools end up in the place of authority.

The *Consequences* Of Being A Nitwit

[8] He who digs a pit may fall into it, and a serpent may bite him who breaks through a wall. [9] He who quarries stones may be hurt by them, and he who splits logs may be endangered by them. [10] If the axe is dull and he does not sharpen its edge, then he must exert more strength. Wisdom has the advantage of giving success. [11] If the serpent bites before being charmed, there is no profit for the charmer – the fool is on a self-destructive path. He lives carelessly and doesn't realize that there are consequences to such an unthinking life. One of the most insightful comedies is the movie Groundhog Day. It is about an arrogant TV weatherman named Phil (Bill Murray) who is assigned to cover the festivities of Groundhog Day in Punxsutawney, Pennsylvania. Due to an unexpected snowstorm, Phil must spend an extra night in this little town with his producer Rita (Andie MacDowell). When Phil awakens the next morning, he discovers it is still

February 2nd. Soon he realizes he is stuck in a 24-hour loop of Groundhog Day. No matter what he does, he wakes up every morning as if nothing had happened the day before. Phil explores what life would be like if there were no consequences. People could do whatever they wanted. He lives recklessly, sparking a police chase. After leaving a swath of destruction, he's arrested. But when Phil wakes up, it is Groundhog Day once again. One day Phil goes out to lunch with Rita. He orders most everything on the menu and lights up a cigarette. Rita asks, "Don't you worry about cholesterol, lung cancer, love-handles?" He says, "I don't worry about anything anymore." She asked, "What makes you so special? Everybody worries about something." Phil contends that he lack any concern over any consequences. But here in the real world, we soon discover that there are consequences to our foolishness.

F. B. Meyers, "This is the bitterest of all – to know that suffering need not have been; that it resulted from one's own indiscretion and inconsistency; that it is the harvest of one's own sowing. Ah me! This is pain!"

The *Characteristics* Of The Nitwit
Their *Language* is foolish

[12] Words from the mouth of a wise man are gracious, while the lips of a fool consume him; [13] the beginning of his talking is folly and the end of it is wicked madness. [14] Yet the fool multiplies words. No man knows what will happen, and who can tell him what will come after him? – someone said, "Never use a gallon of words to express a spoonful of thought."

[19] When there are many words, transgression is unavoidable, But he who restrains his lips is wise. Proverbs 10:19

A crew from the TV show *Mythbusters* was staging an "experiment" in the town of Dublin, California. They were trying to fire a cannon ball into some large water containers at a bomb disposal range. Unfortunately, the *Mythbusters* crew seriously under-estimated the dangerous power of a stray cannonball. According to a newspaper report, "The cantaloupe-sized cannonball missed the water, tore through a cinder-block wall, skipped off a hillside and flew some 700 yards east."

But that didn't end the damage. The cannonball "bounced in front of home on [a quiet street], ripped through the front door, raced up the stairs and blasted through a bedroom .... [Then] it exited the house, leaving a perfectly round hole in the stucco, crossed six-lane Tassajara Road, took out several tiles from the roof of a home on Bellevue Circle and finally slammed into [a family's] beige Toyota minivan in a driveway on Springdale Drive." Regarding the power of the stray cannonball, the owner of the minivan said, "It's shocking—anything could have happened." A spokesmen for the local sheriff's department also commented, "Crazy, crazy, crazy, crazy. You wouldn't think it was possible." Stray words also have tremendous power to rip through communities and lives. Like a cannonball, the fool's multitude of words creates "crazy" damage that you wouldn't think was possible.

Their Labor is futile

The toil of a fool so wearies him that he does not even know how to go to a city – reminds me of when the current had carried away a temporary bridge which Xerxes had made, he became so angry that he ordered lashes to be inflicted on the sea in order to punish it!

The Leadership of the fool is frustrating

* The foolish leader is Immature.

  Woe to you, O land, whose king is a lad - Used in reference to age, it may refer to an infant (Exod 2:6; Judg 13:5; 1 Sam 1:22; 4:21; 2 Sam 12:16), a child just weaned (1 Sam 1:24), an adolescent in puberty (1 Sam 16:11), or a young man of marriageable age (Gen 34:19; 2 Sam 14:21; 18:5, 12). Its technical use denotes "servant" (Num 22:22; Judg 7:10-11; 19:3; 1 Sam 3:9; 2 Sam 16:1; 2 Kgs 4:12, 25; 19:6). When used in reference to rulers, it emphasizes incompetence, naiveté, inexperience, and immaturity (Isa 3:4, 9; 1 Kgs 3:7). We are certainly seeing that in the political realm these days!

* Foolish leaders are incompetent, they lack the experience and judgment to know what is best for the country they serve. The saddest part is that incompetent people think they are competent!

  Researcher Dr. David A. Dunning of Cornell University reports that people who are incompetent are more confident of their abilities than competent people. Dunning and his associate Justin Krueger believe that skills required for competence are the same skills necessary to recognize that ability. Krueger writes in the Journal of Personality and Social Psychology, "Not only do [incompetent people] reach erroneous conclusions and make unfortunate choices, but their incompetence robs them of the ability to realize it." I think we see an example of this in the current leader of North Korea, Kim Jong-un, who clearly has a baby brain to go with his baby face!

* The foolish leader is Intoxicated. *and whose princes feast in the morning.*
[17] *Blessed are you, O land, whose king is of nobility and whose princes eat at the appropriate time—for strength and not for drunkenness* – how sad when leaders present a party type atmosphere. Poor is the country who has fools in the place of leadership, who, first thing in the morning, begin to party; who like children, live to pursue their own pleasures. But how blessed is the country who has wise leaders, who realize that the purpose of eating is simple to give them strength to carry out the tasks of the day."

* The foolish leader is Indifferent.
Through indolence the rafters sag, and through slackness the house leaks – a picture of one who is indifferent to things that need attention. You may remember a few years ago when Snoopy, the loveable beagle in the *Peanuts* cartoon, had his left leg broken. Hundreds wrote letters to Snoopy or sent sympathy cards. Snoopy himself philosophized about his plight one day while perched on top of his doghouse and looking at the huge white cast on his leg. "My body blames my foot for not being able to go places. My foot says it was my head's fault, and my head blamed my eyes.... My eyes say my feet are clumsy, and my right foot says not to blame him for what my left foot did...." Snoopy looks out at his audience and confesses, "I don't say anything because I don't want to get involved." Leaders have a tendency to stick their nose into places where it doesn't belong; and on the other hand to refuse to get involved where they really should.

* The foolish leader is Ignorant.
Men prepare a meal for enjoyment, and wine makes life merry, and money is the answer to everything – today we think money is the answer to every problem we have! The problem is that the Government is quickly running out of money. Even if we had an unlimited supply of money we would soon learn that it is ignorant to think money is the solution to all of our problems! Money has power. But it also has weaknesses. For instance:

Money can buy *land,* but not *love;*
Bonds, but not *brotherhood;*

Gold, but not *gladness;*
Silver, but not *sincerity;*
Hospitals, but not *health;*
Condominiums, but not *character;*
Houses, but not *homes;*
Timber, but not *truth.*
Money can purchase *commodities,* but not *comfort;*

Ranches, but not *righteousness;*
Ships, but not *salvation;*
Hotels, but not *heaven.*
To *save* your money you must *share* it;
To *love* it is to *lose* it;
To *invest* it forever, you must put it in things *eternal.*

Lucy is reading a story to Linus: "And so the king was granted his wish and everything he touched would turn to gold!" Linus jumps to his feet and says, "Stop! You don't have to read any further! I know just what's going to happen." In the final frame he adds, "These things always have a way of backfiring." When something seems too good to be true, it usually is. Sometimes money is not the solution to our problems but the root of our problems.

The *Continuation* Of The Nitwit

This explains why...*Furthermore, in your bedchamber do not curse a king, and in your sleeping rooms do not curse a rich man, for a bird of the heavens will carry the sound and the winged creature will make the matter known* — today with phone tapes, emails, satellites observations, the government has a million and one ways to spy on us. Foolish leadership continues because of intimidation! The Vanity, of having to put up with, Nitwit's. How do we become Nitwit's? Just live life only under the sun! All this reminds me of the Song by Buck Owens, "Act Naturally.

They're gonna put me in the movies
They're gonna make a big star out of me
We'll make a film about a man that's sad and lonely
And all I have to do is act naturally
Well, I hope you come and see me in the movie
Then I'll know that you will plainly see
The biggest fool that ever hit the big time
And all I have to do is act naturally

All any of us have to do to be a Nitwit is to act naturally instead of acting super-naturally by the power of the Holy Spirit unto the glory of God.

CHAPTER 14

Edge of Reality

§

(Not preparing for what's ultimately coming)

I walk along a thin line darling
Dark shadows follow me
Here's where life's dream lies disillusioned
The edge of reality
Oh I can hear strange voices echo
Laughing with mockery
The border line of doom I'm facing
The edge of reality
On the edge of reality she sits there tormenting me
The girl with the nameless face
On the edge of reality where she overpowers me
With fears that I can't explain

She drove me to the point of madness
The brink of misery
If she's not real then I'm condemned to
The edge of reality
On the edge of reality she sits there tormenting me
The girl with the nameless face
On the edge of reality where she overpowers me
With fears that I can't explain

She drove me to the point of madness
The brink of misery
If she's not real then I'm condemned to
The edge of reality
Reality, reality, reality, reality,
Reality, reality, reality, reality
[Recorded: 1968/03/07, first released on single]

THERE IS AN OLD ILLUSTRATION that has a timeless truth to it. It seems a man was asking a young man what he was going to do with his life. He said, "Well first I am going to graduate from high school." The man asked "Then what..." "I think I will go to college and get a degree in Law." "Ok, then what? "I will be a lawyer and eventually hope to become a judge, maybe even get on the Supreme Court." "Then what..." "After many years of service, I guess I'll retire." "Then what?" "I guess eventually I'll die!" "Then what!" The man under the sun usually puts off asking that final "Then what?" And when he does he realizes that he has lived his life in vain. The Vanity of life comes from not preparing for What's ultimately coming at the end of life.

WE PREPARE FOR WHAT'S COMING BY REMEMERING TO GIVE
LET'S TAKE *INVENTORY*

* We can give of our time.

[16] making the most of your time, because the days are evil. Ephesians 5:16 Adrian Rogers, "Time is passing away. This day is passing. I must give an account for this day. I must give an account one day for this sermon that I have preached. Time is such a strange commodity. You can't save it. You can't borrow it. You can't loan it. You can't leave it. You can't take it. You can't give it. All you can do is use it or lose it. Time can't be stopped. In a football game, you can call *time out*. But you can't call *time out* in life. Time can't be stored. You can put your money in the bank, but you can't put your time in the bank. Time can't be

stretched. You can add another cup of water to the soup, but there's no way that you can stretch time. Time can't be shared. I can give you my books, I can give you my money, I can give you my automobile, but I can't give you my time... Someone wrote these words:

When as a child, I laughed and wept, Time crept;

When as a youth, I dreamed and talked, Time walked;
When I became a full-grown man, Time ran;
When older still I daily grew, Time flew;
Soon I shall find in traveling on, Time gone."

   ❋   We can give our *Money*.

[24] "No one can serve two masters; for either he will hate the one and love the other, or he will be devoted to one and despise the other. You cannot serve God and wealth.

Matthew 6:24 (NASB) Mark Twain, "What is the chief end of man?—to get rich. In what way?—dishonestly if we can; honestly if we must. Who is God, the one and only true? Money is God. Gold and Greenbacks and Stock—father, son, and ghosts of same, three persons in one; these are the true and only God, mighty and supreme."

   ❋   We can give our talents and gifts.

[4] Now there are varieties of gifts, but the same Spirit. [5] And there are varieties of ministries, and the same Lord. [6] There are varieties of effects, but the same God who works all things in all *persons*.

[7] But to each one is given the manifestation of the Spirit for the common good. 1 Corinthians 12:4-7. Gifts and talents are strange things – if we do not use them we lose the ability to know how to use them. Some time ago in Reader's Digest there was a short article about a group of sea gulls that was starving to death in St. Augustine. They were not starving because of a food shortage but

because they had forgotten how to fish. For years they had depended on the shrimp fleet operating out of the harbor to toss them scraps from the nets. When the shrimp fleet moved to Key West, they began to starve. They had lost their natural ability to fish because they had not been using it. That was the lesson in the parable of the talents. The servant who did not use the one talent had it taken from him...

* We can give of ourselves.

Rom. 12:1-2. Those confined to under the sun living want to live their life for themselves and then somehow on their death bed offer God what's left! Like the Sunday School teacher who tried to teacher her class the importance of giving their lives to the Lord when they were young and had years of service before them. One teenage girl said, "Well, I want to live my life doing the things I want to do.

After having a good time I will have plenty of time to get serious about serving the Lord.

The next week the teacher bought some beautiful flowers and enjoyed them for several days. After they started to wilt, she waited a few more days and sent them to that teenage girl. With a note, "These flowers were beautiful and I enjoy them for several days. Now that they are almost gone, I thought you might enjoy them!"

Hopefully the teenager got the connection. As we take inventory we find there is a lot that we can give to the Lord. But those living under the sun don't understand the value of living for God and eternity. Willie Nelson is now an old man and will one day learn the truth that we reap only what we sow. He had made millions of dollars but has not spent it wisely or godly or even legally. A few years ago he ended up owing the IRS 16.7 million dollars in taxes and penalties. Robert Draper, "Financial planning, of course, that had no place in Willie's worldview. His belief is that, you should spend your way through life and die a pauper, has kept him forever at odds with his money men." Willie once told his financial adviser, "It's more fun if we don't plan!" The problem is that one day there will be a divine audit for which we must give an account.

Therefore we also have as our ambition, whether at home or absent, to be pleasing to Him. [10] For we must all appear before the judgment seat of Christ, so that each one may be recompensed for his deeds in the body, according to what he has done, whether good or bad. 2 Corinthians 5:9-10

GIVE EXPECTANTLY

* A Demand

We should Give *Expectantly*. It begins with a simple demand in those words, Cast your bread - The verb נ֖ש (*shalakh*, "to send; to cast") refers to the action of sending something to someone. The verb is an *imperative* mood which is a command; the *piel* stem is the intensive form, thus translated cast or aggressively throw.

* The Daring

your bread on the surface of the waters – The "cast your bread" line, though it sounds odd today, was understood in Solomon's day.

It refers to doing business in grain by putting it on a ship and having it set sail to be traded—casting it on the waters. You harvest your crop, send it off to sell it, and then receive back a dividend. This was risky in that there were pirates, shipwrecks, and unscrupulous traders. But the only way to get that financial return is to take the risk. It is also possible that he has in mind the practice of casting the grain, not into the river, but on the flood-plain waters in the annual river overflow, such as in the Nile River valley. When the flood waters subsided, then the grain would settle into the rich soils of the flood plain, and eventually yield an abundant harvest.

* The Declaration

for you will find it – the principle is that the result of giving is receiving. There will be a return blessing. This is the same principle laid out in 2 Cor. 9:6-11. We might say what goes around, comes around – and it is not just related to money. Less known than his Aunt Corrie Ten Boom, Peter was part of the ten Boom family that provided a safe house in Haarlem, the Netherlands, to which Jewish people escaped during the Nazi occupation.

Peter and others extricated hundreds of Jewish children from orphanages ahead of the S.S. troops, who were collecting them to ship to concentration camps. Peter also played the organ in a country church. Though it was forbidden by German decree, one Sunday Peter pulled out the stops and played the Dutch national anthem, while shocked but proud churchgoers stood and sang the words. For this act of defiance, Peter, then 16, went to prison. After the war, Peter went around the world with the same message as his famous aunt: that forgiveness is the only answer to hatred. In Israel on one of his tours, he suffered a heart attack. Prompt surgery was essential to save his life. The cardiologist spoke with his patient before the operation. "I see your name is ten Boom. Are you by any chance related to the ten Booms of Haarlem?" "Yes," replied Peter. "That's my family." The doctor replied, "And I'm one of the babies your family saved!"

✤   But we also have the Delay

It comes back only *after many days* – we do not sow and reap in the same day! If we sow our goods as God directs us in this life, we will reap benefits when eternity dawns. I couldn't help think of the missionary who received a letter from home, as she opened it, a ten dollar bill fell out. She was delighted but not long afterwards as she looked out the widow she noticed a shabbily dressed man sitting on the corner not far from her house. Moved with compassion she went out and gave him the ten dollar bill and said, *"Don't Despair!"* The next day there was a knock on her door, there was the same man. He handed her a wad of money! She asked, "What is this for?" And he said, "Lady, Don't Despair, paid off 100 to one!" This verse is true of the gospel. We may not see immediate results as we share the bread of life, but the eventual harvest is sure.

GIVE GENEROUSLY

Divide your portion to seven, or even to eight – this speaks of giving generously. Robert Russell tells about a handful of our people went on a mission trip to Eastern Europe several weeks ago. When they came back, they told of the dedication of the Christians in Romania. "Christians there don't have very much, but they believe they should tithe. They think that's God's standard. But the government of Romania is repressive, and they are allowed to give only 2.5 percent of their income to charitable organizations.

They're trying to minimize the opportunity for any anti-government organization. So Romanians are searching for loopholes in the law, so that they'll be able to give 10 percent. The Romanian Christians have less, and they're looking for a way to give 10 percent." By contrast we have more, and we're free to give as we please. In fact, we get a tax break by doing so, and yet many are looking for loopholes in the Scripture to avoid doing it. I have heard it all, tithing is legalistic, it is Old Testament, etc.

GIVE URGENTLY

for you do not know what misfortune may occur on the earth – we do not know when the day will come when we will not be able to give. Giving is an opportunity that is not always afforded a person. This is a principle I have observed often – people for example refuse to go to church, then they get sick and they cannot go to church…I have seen people with good jobs and large paychecks but refuse to give, then they lose their jobs and can barely feed themselves…Somebody said, "Four things cannot come back: the spoken word, the spend arrow, time past, and the neglected opportunity."

GIVE CONTINUALLY

Yes, even though life is Uncertain. An Illustration. *If the clouds are full, they pour out rain upon the earth; and whether a tree falls toward the south or toward the north, wherever the tree falls, there it lies*– a storm can bring needed rain but it may also knock over valuable trees and do much damage. The Application. *He who watches the wind will not sow and he who looks at the clouds will not reap* – keep on sowing in spite of life's uncertainty. You surely cannot reap if you do not sow because you're concerned about what will happen.

MacDonald, "If you wait till conditions are perfect, you will accomplish nothing. There are usually some wind and some clouds. If you wait for zero wind conditions, you will never get the seed into the fields. If you wait until there is no risk of rain, the crops will rot before they are harvested. The man who waits for certainty will wait forever." Give even though things are Unknown. The Examples given is we do not know the path the wind will take, *Just as you do not know the path of the wind;* and we do not know the formation of a baby - *and how bones are formed in the womb of the pregnant woman, so you do not know the activity of God who makes all things.* The Principle is *so you do not know the activity of God who makes all things* - God's ways are mysterious to us…And all of this is to be continual, *Sow your seed in the morning and do not be idle in the evening, for you do not know whether morning or evening sowing will succeed, or whether both of them alike will be good* – by faith just keep giving regardless of what life seems to bring.

Courson, "We find ourselves saying, "As soon as I get a better job" or "as soon as we pay off the credit card bill" or "as soon as we get our yard planted, then we'll really share…There is never a good time to give. If you're waiting for a more convenient time, it will never come. So do it now. Now is the time to do whatever the Lord has placed upon your heart… Keep giving because you don't know which seed will sprout. Keep sowing in the morning; keep reaching out in the evening. There really is no easy time to write that check, to give generously of whatever resources you have."

We need to Give even when life turns Unpleasant, there is a comforting factor, *The light is pleasant, and it is good for the eyes to see the sun.* [8] *Indeed, if a man should live many years, let him rejoice in them all* – God in his mercy gives each of us many years of good days. While we focus on our sick days, we often forget our healthy years! As well as a candid fact, and let him remember the days of darkness, for they will be many. Everything that is to come *will be* futility – days of darkness are coming. We prepare for What is coming by remembering to Give – expectantly; generously; urgently; and consistently regardless of lives uncertainty. We were made to give, and when God knows that we understand that principle He makes sure that we receive. Mike Herman, "I've been going to professional baseball games and trying to get a souvenir baseball as far back as I can remember. A foul ball, a home run ball, or even a batting practice ball—anything would do. I was taking in batting practice for the St. Louis Cardinals, and as I watched Mark McGwire and his teammates, I got to know a five-year-old boy who was also trying to get a ball. His name was James.

He tried hard to pronounce the players' names as he politely asked for a ball: "Mr. Timwin (Timlin), can I have a ball, please?" Before I knew it, my mission became getting a ball for James. For about 20 minutes, I told him the names of the players who had a ball near the fence we stood behind, and the players turned and smiled as James tried to say their names. Still, no ball. Finally I told James he could have my ball if I caught one (I had been unsuccessful in catching a ball for almost 28 years, so that felt like a safe promise). Five minutes later. I caught a ball, and yes, I gave it to James. I wonder how often God waits to give us something until we are willing to give it away?" But someone who leaves God out and eternity has little motivation to give. Self-centered people try to prepare for the future by saving, getting, and hoarding, and thus are not prepared for what is coming.

WE PREPARE FOR WHAT IS COMING BY REMEMBERING GOD

Living Irresponsible means focusing on that which is Pleasant. *Rejoice, young man, during your childhood and let your heart be pleasant during the days of young manhood_–* only do that which you find pleasant. If we follow the Impulses of our heart, as he says, *follow the impulses of your heart and the desires of your eyes –* in other words do as we please! We can be sure an unpleasant day of accountability is coming - *Yet know that God will bring you to judgment for all these things…because childhood and the prime of life are fleeting –* and that day is right around the corner. "Young people feel invincible. So, in the years of their greatest strength, it is difficult to fathom that the time will come when their vigor is diminished or even gone. They assume, though perhaps subconsciously, that the energy and drive they enjoy today will continue through the end of life, that the opportunities that youthful energy and ability provide will always be available…Solomon offers wise counsel specifically aimed at those who are younger. In essence, his counsel is this: make the most of your productive years while you can, while you have the physical stamina and strength to do so. The time will come—sooner than you can imagine—when these physical abilities will wane. You will reap in old age what you have sown in youth." [Preachers Outline and Bible sermons]. The understanding the need to live Responsibly. *So, remove grief and anger from your heart and put away pain from your body* — we should remove needless sorrow. We do not prepare for what is coming when we forget to remember God.

"He brushed his teeth three times a day,
He wore his rubbers when it rained,

He never exceeded the speed limit,
He never forgot to buckle his seat belt.
He made only one mistake.
He forgot God!"

The vanity of life comes when we do not prepare for what is coming by not remembering to Give and not remembering God. We would all do well to answer that last "Then what?" long before it comes upon us.

"Across the fields of yesterday
He sometimes comes to me
The little lad just back from play
The boy I used to be.
He smiles at me so wishfully

When once he's crept within
It is as though he had hoped to see
The man I might have been."

Reality check:

* First what we might have been is still far below the perfection God demands! This, what we might have been mentality, is in reality a mirage.
* The only perfect man who ever lived was Jesus Christ, and He is our life! This of course does not mean that
* there is not loss of rewards and accountability for our lives.

CHAPTER 15
I Feel so bad

§

Weariness of growing old and Where it leads)

Feel so bad
Like a ball game on a rainy day
Feel so bad
Like a ball game on a rainy day
Yes' I got my rain check
Shake my head and walk away

Oooo-people that's the way I feel
Oooo-people that's the way I feel
Sometimes I think I want
Then again I think I don't
Sometimes I want to stay here
Then again I want to leave here
Then again I want to stay
Yes, I got my train fare
Pack my grip and ride away

Oooo-people that's the way I feel
Oooo-people that's the way I feel
Sometimes I think I want
Then again I think I don't

[Recorded: 1961/03/12, first released on single]

A LETTERS FROM BRUCE AND Rose Bliven that appeared in Ann Landers's column:

"At 86, Rose and I live by the rules of the elderly: If the toothbrush is wet, you have brushed your teeth. If the bedside radio is warm in the morning, you left it on all night. If you are wearing one brown shoe and one black shoe, you have a pair just like it somewhere in the closet. Try not to mind when a friend tells you on your birthday that a case of prune juice has been donated in you name to a retirement home. I stagger when I walk, and small boys follow me making bets on which way I'll go next. This upsets me. Children shouldn't gamble. Like most elderly people, we spend many happy hours in front of the TV set. We rarely turn it on. One of the vanities of life is growing old, if you're not living with eternity in mind, growing old under the sun can become unbearable. Vanity comes from the Weariness of growing old and where it leads.

AVOID THE DECEPTION OF YOUTH ABOUT THE CERTAINTY OF OLD AGE

Remember God has the Right to Rule. *Remember also your Creator in the days of your youth* – the author of our life obviously has the right to rule our life! The time to serve the Lord is when we are young and have the energy, health, time, and opportunity to do so. In his book *Don't Waste Your Life*, John Piper recounts a story his father often told in his days as a fiery Baptist evangelist. It is the story of a man who came to saving faith in Jesus Christ near the end of his earthly existence. Piper writes:

"The church had prayed for this man for decades. He was hard and resistant. But this time, for some reason, he showed up when my father was preaching. At the end of the service, during a hymn, to everyone's amazement he came and took my father's hand. They sat down together on the front pew of the church as the people were dismissed. God opened his heart to the Gospel of Christ, and he was saved from his sins and given eternal life. But that did not stop him from sobbing and saying, as the tears ran down his wrinkled face, "I've wasted it! I've wasted it!"

By the grace of God, even a life that is almost totally wasted can still be redeemed. But why wait even a moment longer before starting to serve Jesus? You have only one life to live. Don't waste it by living for yourself when you can use it instead for the glory of God. Also Remember that time is Running out, we are exhorted to do things *before the evil days come* – talking about the days of old age which end in death. Life is racing by and before we know it our youth will be a thing of the past. I have never been one to watch soap operas but I do remember one of them after the theme music has played for a moment; one has an announcer who says, "*Like sands through the hour glass, so are the days of our lives.*" It speaks of the profound truth that life is short and is quickly coming to an end.

[6]"My days are swifter than a weaver's shuttle, And come to an end without hope. [7]"Remember that my life is *but* breath; My eye will not again see good. Job 7:6-7

[1]"Man, who is born of woman, Is short-lived and full of turmoil. [2]"Like a flower he comes forth and withers. He also flees like a shadow and does not remain. Job 14:1-2

[5] "Behold, You have made my days *as* handbreadths, And my lifetime as nothing in Your sight; Surely every man at his best is a mere breath. Selah. Psalm 39:5

[47] Remember what my span of life is; For what vanity You have created all the sons of men! [48] What man can live and not see death? Can he deliver his soul from the power of Sheol? Selah. Psalm 89:47-48

[14] Yet you do not know what your life will be like tomorrow. You are *just* a vapor that appears for a little while and then vanishes away. James 4:14

A man came rushing up to a ferry, breathless after running at a terrific pace, but he got there just as the gateman shut the door in his face. A bystander remarked, "You didn't run fast enough." The disappointed man answered, "I ran fast enough, but I didn't start on time." To accomplish the most for God in a lifetime, you must start in early—"in the days of your youth"

The Deterration Of Old Age Is Coming

The Pleasure of the elderly — none!

He says, *and the years draw near when you will say, "I have no delight in them"* — this may seem like an overstatement but if you leave God and eternity out growing old is fill with pain and little pleasure. The truth is there is very little pleasure in life, when God is left out of it, regardless of how old we are. Yes there is pleasure in sin for a season, but as any hunter can tell you a season doesn't last very long. Seeking pleasure without God reminds me of something I read the other day. In New York City, there are eight million cats and eleven million dogs. New York City is basically just concrete and steel, so when you have a pet in New York City and it dies, you can't just go out in the back yard and bury it. The city authorities decided that for $50 they would dispose of your deceased pet for you. One lady was enterprising. She thought, *I can render a service to people in the city and save them money.* She placed an ad in the newspaper that said, "When your pet dies, I will come and take care of the carcass for you for $25." This lady would go to the local Salvation Army and buy an old suitcase for two dollars. Then when someone would call about his or her pet, she would go to the home and put the deceased pet in the suitcase. She would then take a ride on the subway, where there are thieves. She would set the suitcase down, and she would act like she wasn't watching. A thief would come by and steal her suitcase. She'd look up and say, "Wait. Stop. Thief." My guess is the people who stole those suitcases got a real surprise when they got home. A lot of us are like those New York thieves. We're chasing after pleasure, and we grab what we think will give it to us; however, when we get it, it doesn't quite deliver. With old age everything intensifies – especially pain!

THE PLIGHT OF THE ELDERLY
How Do You Know When You're Getting Old?

* Everything hurts, and what doesn't hurt, doesn't work.
* You sit in a rocking chair but can't get it going.
* You look forward to a dull evening.
* Your little black book contains names ending only in "M.D."
* Your children begin to look middle-aged.
* You dim the lights for economic reasons, rather than romantic ones.

* You sink your teeth into a steak, and they stay there.
* Your back goes out more than you do.
* The little gray haired lady you help across the street is your wife.
* Most of your dreams are reruns.

THE DREARY DAYS OF OLD AGE

before the sun and the light, the moon and the stars are darkened, and clouds return after the rain; - this is figurative language which seems to be describing the end of the world. It is figurative language speaking about old age or perhaps death. Death has already been presented as darkness in this book. The immediate context seems to suggest that growing old under the sun brings forth dark days. Clouds coming back after the rain speak of more rain. Life can seem like one storm after another.

THE DAYS OF MUSCLE DETERIORATION

in the day that the watchmen of the house tremble — speaking of the hands. You begin to feel the pain of arthritis in them; you no longer have a strong grip - you have trouble opening those child proof bottles, they no longer pass the jar your way that nobody can open, and things like buttoning and unbuttoning become a major effort.

[2] "Indeed, what *good was* the strength of their hands to me? Vigor had perished from them. Job 30:2

President Dwight Eisenhower described his mother as a smart and saintly lady. "Often in this job I've wished I could consult her. But she is in heaven. However, many times I have felt I knew what she would say." One night in their farm home, Mrs. Eisenhower was playing a card game with her boys. "Now, don't get me wrong," said the former president, "it was not with those cards that have kings, queens, jacks, and spades on them. Mother was too straitlaced for that." President Eisenhower said the game they were playing was called Flinch. "Anyway, Mother was the dealer, and she dealt me a very bad hand. I began to complain. Mother said, 'Boys, put down your cards. I want to say something, particularly to Dwight. You are in a game in your home with your mother and brothers who love you. But out in the world you will be dealt bad hands without love. Here is some advice for you boys. Take those bad hands without complaining and play them out. Ask God to help you, and you will win the important game called life." The president added, "I've tried to follow that wise advice always." When we enter into old age life usually deals us very bad hands! [Yes, that was a joke, lighten up…] The legs start to lose their strength and the back

DAYS OF DROOPING OVER

and mighty men stoop – it's hard to believe but people actually shrink as they get older! The legs start to lose their strength and the back starts looking questionable. Janice Walsh, "After receiving the news that our son had been born, both sets of grandparents arrived at the hospital together. Just getting out of the car was quite an ordeal since all four were in various stages of recovery from knee operations and hip replacements. As the foursome hobbled towards the hospital entrance, brandishing canes and walkers, my mother quipped, "Mercy! I hope they don't admit us before we get to the maternity ward."

DAYS OF DIMINISHED TEETH

the grinding ones stand idle because they are few – because there are so few teeth, chewing is no longer an option. Reminds me of something Matthew Thomas Jr. shared, "As my grandmother and I were walking towards the United Nations Building in New York City, we came upon a street evangelist who was trying to get the attention of passersby. He urged those near him to flee from the wrath to come. "I warn you," he roared, "that there will be weeping, and wailing, and gnashing of teeth!" An old woman in the crowd shouted snidely: "Sir, I have no teeth!" "Lady," the evangelist retorted, "teeth will be provided!"

DAYS WHERE EYES GROW DIM

and those who look through windows grow dim – you go to the store and find that you can no longer read the information on things; you beginning looking for that Giant Print Bible; and you play trombone every time you read the newspaper. Joseph Bayly, delightful personal friend now in heaven, was flying from Chicago to the city of Los Angeles. He engaged the woman sitting next to him in conversation. She was a little over 40, well dressed, and quite articulate. He asked,

"Where are you from?" She said, "From Palm Springs." Knowing Palm Springs to be a city of the rich and famous, he asked, "What's Palm Springs like?" Being perceptive, she answered, "Palm

Springs is a beautiful place filled with unhappy people." Taking advantage of the occasion, he pressed the question, "Are you unhappy?" She said, "Yes, I certainly am." "Why?" he asked. She said, "I can answer it in one word, and that word is mortality. Until I was 40, I had perfect eyesight. Shortly after, I went to the doctor because I couldn't see as well as I could before. Ever since that time, these corrective glasses have been a sign to me that not only are my eyes wearing out, but I'm wearing out. Some day I'm going to die. I really haven't been happy since that time." If losing our eyesight confronts us with the reality that death is a certainty, and somehow gets us to be receptive to the gospel it will be a great blessing.

DAYS OF NEAR DEAFNESS

and the doors on the street are shut as the sound of the grinding mill is low… and all the daughters of song will sing softly — you almost just automatically ask people to repeat themselves, and talking to someone on the phone makes you feel like an idiot because you can only understand about one out of every four words.

[34] But Barzillai said to the king, "How long have I yet to live, that I should go up with the king to Jerusalem? [35] "I am now eighty years old. Can I distinguish between good and bad? Or can your servant taste what I eat or what I drink? Or can I hear anymore the voice of singing men and women? Why then should your servant be an added burden to my lord the king? 2 Samuel 19:34-35

Reminds me of the elderly couple who were sitting on their porch. Both were almost deaf. He said, "Dear, I love you!" She yells back, "What?" He said, "I love you!" She replies, "I'm sick of you too!" Days when you feel like you've taken a bottle of No Dose when you haven't! It goes on to say, *and one will arise at the sound of the bird* — The contrast is amusing, one has trouble hearing and yet is awakened by the sound of a bird chirping. For one thing as we get older we start to get tired by 9:00 pm, so we go to bed or doze off in an easy chair. As a result are wide awake by 4:00 am.

DAYS OF DREAD

Furthermore, men are afraid of a high place and of terrors on the road – when you're young and fall you just bounce back up.

But the older you get the harder it is to recover from a fall. The elderly cannot protect themselves as they could in their younger days and such vulnerability produces fear.

DAYS OF DISCOLORED HAIR

the almond tree blossoms – the almond tree gives off white blossoms. Of course most elderly are thrilled just to have hair! But it is a little scary to see it all turning white and if you grow a bead you feel like you're playing Santa Clause twelve months out of the year. A woman was sitting in the waiting room for her first appointment with a new dentist. She noticed his DDS diploma, which bore his full name. Suddenly, she remembered that a tall, handsome, dark-haired boy with the same name had been in her high school class so many years ago. *Could this be the same guy I had a crush on way back then?* she wondered. She quickly discarded any such thought when she met the balding, gray-haired man with the deeply lined face. *He's way too old to have been my classmate,* she thought to herself. Still, after he examined her teeth, she asked, "Did you happen to attend Morgan Park High School?" "Yes! I'm a Mustang," he gleamed with pride. "When did you graduate?" she asked. "1959," he replied. "Why do you ask?" "You were in my class!" she exclaimed. "Really?" he said, looking at her closely. "What did you teach?"

DAYS OF DRAGGING YOURSELF ABOUT

the grasshopper drags himself along – so many activities you used to do, you can only do in slow motion or not at all. Speed is no longer an option.

DAYS WHEN DESIRES FAIL

and the caperberry is ineffective – the meaning of the noun is uncertain, it occurs only once in the Old Testament. Its root suggests desire, but an alternative is "the caperberry," a small fruit that supposedly stimulates the appetite. Jewish tradition took the term to refer to sexual desire. Solomon says things just won't work the way they used to. Even today, Viagra doesn't always do the trick!

J. Vernon McGee, "Solomon will paint a picture of old age, and it is not a pretty picture. Nevertheless, it is your picture and my picture in old age. When I first preached on this chapter of Ecclesiastes, I was a very young preacher, and I wondered if it would really be like this. Now I am here to testify that the description of old age in Ecclesiastes is accurate."

City Slickers recounts the adventures of three friends having mid-life crises. They escape the city and head west for a two-week cattle run to discover what's important in life. Before they leave, Mitch (played by Billy Crystal) shares what he does for a living at Dad's Day at his son's school. Instead of talking about his work as a salesman, Mitch bewilders the third graders with a monologue about how bleak their future is. He says:

Value this time in your life, kids, because this is the time in your life when you still have your choices, and it goes by so quickly. When you're a teenager, you think you can do anything, and you do.

Your 20s are a blur.

Your 30s, you raise your family, you make a little money, and you think to yourself, *what happened to my 30s?*

Your 40s, you grow a little pot belly. You grow another chin. The music starts to get too loud, and one of your old girlfriends from high school becomes a grandmother.

Your 50s, you have a minor surgery. You'll call it a procedure, but it's a surgery.

Your 60s, you have a major surgery; the music is still loud, but it doesn't matter because you can't hear it anyway.

70s, you and the wife retire to Fort Lauderdale. You start eating dinner at 2:00, lunch around 10:00, breakfast the night before. And you spend most of your time wandering around malls looking for the ultimate in soft yogurt and muttering, "How come the kids don't call?"

By your 80s, you've had a major stroke, and you end up babbling to some Jamaican nurse who your wife can't stand but who you call mama.

Any questions?

THE DESTINATION OF OLD AGE

DEATH

For man goes to his eternal home while mourners go about in the street [6] *Remember Him before the silver cord is broken and the golden bowl is crushed, the pitcher by the well is shattered and the wheel at the cistern is crushed* – "We do not know precisely what the images of broken cords, bowls, pitchers, and wheels refer to. However, verse 7 is very clear; dust goes back to dust and the spirit goes to God. So there can be little doubt that the images of brokenness in verse 6 points to death as well." For those who leave God out of the picture death is not only inevitable but fearful! Since its birth in 1947, the world's eyes have been on the famous Doomsday Clock. This symbolic timepiece measures how close the world is to "midnight"—that is, a nuclear or environmental apocalypse. It is officially set by the *Bulletin of the Atomic Scientists* magazine, a resource dedicated to educating the world about global security. The magazine made news in 2007 when physicists collectively decided to set the clock ahead two minutes to 11:55 pm. The jump forward was in response to the continued dangers of on going wars, the worldwide increase in nuclear weapons, and the ever-growing threat of climate change. The closest the Doomsday Clock has ever been to midnight was two minutes, when the U.S. successfully tested a hydrogen bomb in 1953. The furthest it has been from midnight was 17 minutes, after the 1991 fall of the Soviet Union. We talk about the end of the world being closer or farther away, but if you're in your late 70's your Doomsday Clock is about to strike midnight. We did not determine our birthday and we will not determine our death day either – One doctor told his patient, "I'm afraid you only have three weeks to live." "Okay then," the patient replied, "I'll take the last two weeks of July and the week between Christmas and New Year's." It doesn't work like that...

DUST

then the dust will return to the earth as it was – Gen. 3:19

February 7 is the day Sinclair Lewis was born in 1885 at Saulk Center, Minnesota. Lewis won the Nobel Prize for Literature in 1930. His best known works of social satire were *Main Street, It Can't Happen Here* and *Babbit*. Yet, for all his renown and wealth, Lewis died in Rome of alcoholism. Upon his death in 1951, he was cremated and his ashes sent to Rome's U.S. Embassy for disposition. One morning a visitor noticed a worker on her knees with a dustpan and broom. Next to her was an overturned funerary urn. When asked what she was doing, she replied nonchalantly, "Sweeping up Sinclair Lewis." If we focus on the words, "sweeping up Sinclair Lewis," we realize the abject futility of the human experience outside of the soul and its relationship to God. This is why the Bible says: "For he knows how we are formed, he remembers that we are dust. But from everlasting to everlasting the LORD's love is with those who fear him" (Psalm 103:14, 17).

DEPARTURE

<u>and the spirit will return to God who gave it</u> – everybody ultimately returns to God either as Savior or as Judge. We can appear before the Judgment Seat of Christ or the Great White Throne.

THE DECLARATION OF OLD AGE AND WHERE IT LEADS FROM AN UNDER THE SUN PERSPECTIVE.

"Vanity of vanities," says the Preacher, *"all is vanity!"* The vanity of life is seen in the Weariness that old age brings. The flip side is that when we practice the presence of God and live this life with eternity in mind old age is a blessing to ourselves and to others. In August of 2006, *Newsweek* magazine profiled the lives of Ruth and Billy Graham—not their historic evangelistic crusades and international impact, but their life as an elderly couple approaching their final chapters on earth. One thing that shone brilliantly through the pages of the article was the incredible quality of their marriage. Billy said, "At night we have time together, we pray together and read the Bible together every night. It's a wonderful period of life for both of us. We've never had a love like we do now—we feel each other's hearts." He said, "I think about heaven a great deal, I think about the failures in my life in the past, but know they have been covered

by the blood of Christ. And that gives me a great sense of confidence. I have a certainty about eternity that is a wonderful thing and I thank God for giving me that certainty. I do not fear death. I may fear a little bit about the process, but not death itself, because I think the moment that my spirit leaves this body, I will be in the presence of the Lord."

CHAPTER 16

Happy Ending

§

(The Way the book ends)

Happy ending, happy ending
Give me a story with a, happy ending
When boy meets girl and then
They never part again
But live forever happily, like you and me

Our love story gets me so upset
Like Romeo, and Juliet
I'm not smart enough to figure why
Some folks enjoy, a real good cry

Happy ending, happy ending
Give me a story with a, happy ending
When boy meets girl and then
They never part again
But live forever happily, like you and me

Never thought that I would stand a chance
That you'd give me, a second glance
But I think that you can play the part
And give a guy, a happy heart

Happy ending, happy ending
Give me a story with a, happy ending
When boy meets girl and then

They never part again
But live forever happily, like you and me
When boy meets girl and then, they never part again

but live forever happily, like you and me

Like you and me, like you and me
Like you and me
[Recorded: 1962/08/30, first released on It Happened At The World's Fair]

Mrs. Einstein, married to Albert Einstein—they say the most intelligent man who ever lived; Somebody once asked her, "Mrs. Einstein, do you understand the theory of relativity?" She said, "No, but I understand Dr. Einstein." We do not understand the mysteries of the universe, but we can know God and live life with eternity in mind. The Summation of the book of Ecclesiastes.

The Wisdom Of Solomon

* His Perception. *In addition to being a wise man, the Preacher also taught the people knowledge* - outside of the Lord Jesus, Solomon was the wisest man that ever lived (1 Ki. 3:3-28). Here probably wisdom and knowledge are used as parallels. Knowledge means "skill or perception." And it is the fear of the Lord which is the beginning of knowledge (Prov. 1:7).
* His Pondering, *and he pondered* – he weighed and evaluated, and carefully thought out things.
* His Pursuits. He *searched out* – he studied and examined these things. He has done one experiment after another to show us how empty life is when we leave God out of our lives.

* His Proverbs. *and arranged many proverbs* – there are many proverbs in this book and of course their Solomon also wrote the book of Proverbs. These are pithy wise sayings and teachings.

In a day of half truths it's refreshing that Solomon took the time to study his message thoroughly and accurately. In fact the entire Bible is completely trustworthy and reliable. An article on NPR's (National Public Radio's) website lists 12 common half-truths that many of us have accepted as facts. For instance, various news organizations have pointed out that Subway's $5 foot long sandwich actually measures 11 inches instead of 12. (Subway has explained that their methods of baking the bread can cause a slight size differential.) Here are a few more half-truths the article:

* A <u>koala bear</u> is not a bear; it's a marsupial.
* A <u>palm tree</u> is not a tree. Palm trees belong to the monocot family of flowering plants, which also includes grasses and grains.
* "<u>Swollen glands</u>" are not actually glands; they are a series of lymph nodes.
* A <u>mountain goat</u> is not really a goat.
* <u>Pink</u> is not exactly a color. Physicists claim that pink should really be called "minus green" because "pink" is just the leftovers of white light when you take out the green.

Solomon's Sermons were well researched and accurate.

THE WORDS OF SOLOMON
HIS WORDS WERE DELIGHTFUL
The Preacher sought to find delightful words - The basic meaning is to feel great favor towards something. The noun ḥēpeṣ is used more frequently, thirty-nine times, and in varying contexts.

It is used in such expressions as "land of delight" (<u>Malachi 3:12</u>) or "words of delight" (<u>Eccles. 12:10</u>), where it speaks of the pleasure which the "land" or "words" give. I have always enjoyed reading the book of Ecclesiastes, it gives a perspective on things that you can't get anywhere else. It sort of shows what a crocked stick is like, so you appreciate the value of a straight one.

His words were Truthful. *and to write words of truth correctly* – what he wrote was upright and true (NIV).

HIS WORDS WERE MOTIVATIONAL

* *The words of wise men are like goads and masters of these collections are like well-driven nails* – a goad was a sharp stick used to stir cattle to action. This book motivates one to reevaluate one's goals in life (Ac.26:14). The well-driven nails are parallel to the goads. It is common to find the second line expanding or giving more detail to the first line. The nails add a description to the goads. Apparently the goads have nails sticking out of them; they are well driven or firmly fixed so they can do the job of moving the animal effectively.

HIS WORDS WERE INSPIRATIONAL

they are given by one Shepherd – the question before us is who is this shepherd? Some take it to be a reference to Solomon since kings are referred to as shepherds. Others believe it is talking about God Himself, and even take the liberty of using a capital letter. Others believe that it is just a general reference to a shepherd. I like to think of it as being a reference to God who is the One giving Solomon these words (2 Tim. 3:16-17). But of course the text does not make this view a certainty. One thing for sure these, like all Scripture, are wonderful words from which we can profit greatly from. I think it is delightful how many different kinds of scripture there are – you can read History or Poetry or Biography or Prophecy or whatever!_One of the marvels of the Internet age is a thing called Pandora radio. When you listen to a radio station on terrestrial or satellite radio, you have to listen to every song played. You can change the channel, but you can't change the song. You're stuck with whatever you're given. But that's not so on Pandora. On Pandora, you put in different singers, bands, or songs that you like; and they use an algorithm to parse the music that you list. And by each song that's played Pandora puts a little thumbs-up sign and a little thumbs-down sign. When you click the thumbs-up sign, the algorithm is strengthened even more to your tastes, and it will play more music like that. If you click the thumbs-down sign, Pandora will just skip that particular song and bring up a different one for you to judge. Well the entire Bible is thumbs-up! But sometimes I want to read sheer doctrine and find myself delighting in the Epistles; other times I'm in the mood to read the thrilling narrations found in much of the Old Testament; the other day I just wanted to read the Song of Solomon. The inspired material is virtually limitless!

THE WARNING OF SOLOMON
WRITING IS ENDLESS
But beyond this, my son, be warned: the writing of many books is endless — This is what every publisher wants to hear! I have never written a book and probably never will, but I have written many sermons throughout my years of ministry.

READING BRINGS WEARINESS.
and excessive devotion to books is wearying to the body — This is what every student knows! I have books in my study at the church, in my study at the house, in my closets, under the bed — I have books in my computer. I love to read and yet it can get tiring after burning the midnight oil night after night. Wiersbe, "The statement is a warning to the student not to go beyond what God has written in His Word. Indeed, there are many books, and studying them can be a wearisome chore. But don't permit man's books to rob you of God's wisdom. "Be warned, my son, of anything in addition to them [the words of the wise]" (v. 12, niv). These "nails" are sure and you can depend on them. Don't test God's truth by the "many books" written by men; test men's books by the truth of God's Word."

THE WHOLE OF WHAT SOLOMON IS SAYING.

THERE SHOULD BE REVERENCE

The conclusion, when all has been heard, is: fear God – this is all you really need!

"It is the LORD of hosts whom you should regard as holy. And He shall be your fear, And He shall be your dread.

Isaiah 8:13

[16] Better is a little with the fear of the LORD Than great treasure and turmoil with it. Proverbs 15:16

[28] "Do not fear those who kill the body but are unable to kill the soul; but rather fear Him who is able to destroy both soul and body in hell. Matthew 10:28

[31] So the church throughout all Judea and Galilee and Samaria enjoyed peace, being built up; and going on in the fear of the Lord and in the comfort of the Holy Spirit, it continued to increase. Acts 9:31

Therefore, having these promises, beloved, let us cleanse ourselves from all defilement of flesh and spirit, perfecting holiness in the fear of God. 2 Corinthians 7:1

Honor all people, love the brotherhood, fear God, honor the king. 1 Peter 2:17

I am sure most of us have done some frog hunting in our day. If you have you soon discover they have an amazing ability to elude being captured. I read that the frog's optical field of perception is like a blackboard wiped clean, and that the only images it receives are objects that directly concern him—such as his natural enemies or the food he needs for survival. Therefore these amphibious little creatures are never distracted by unimportant things, but are aware only of essentials and whatever may be dangerous to them. We can learn a valuable lesson from these creatures – instead of allowing ourselves to be preoccupied with things under the sun, let's fix our attention on which really matters. That would be God Himself!

THERE SHOULD BE OBEDIENCE

and keep His commandments – when we truly fear God, we will obey Him.

He said, "Do not stretch out your hand against the lad, and do nothing to him; for now I know that you fear God, since you have not withheld your son, your only son, from Me." Genesis 22:12 See Deut. 13:4, etc.

[8] The LORD said to Satan, "Have you considered My servant Job? For there is no one like him on the earth, a blameless and upright man, fearing God and turning away from evil."

Job 1:8

[20] Moses said to the people, "Do not be afraid; for God has come in order to test you, and in order that the fear of Him may remain with you, so that you may not sin." Exodus 20:20

[3] "The God of Israel said, The Rock of Israel spoke to me, 'He who rules over men righteously, Who rules in the fear of God, 2 Samuel 23:3

[6] By lovingkindness and truth iniquity is atoned for, And by the fear of the LORD one keeps away from evil. Proverbs 16:6

[22] Slaves, in all things obey those who are your masters on earth, not with external service, as those who *merely* please men, but with sincerity of heart, fearing the Lord. Colossians 3:22

Real reverence always leads to a life of obedience...

Lee Eclov, "I used to think that living in "the fear of the Lord" is like driving down the street while watching the policeman in your rearview mirror. But actually there's a better picture for the fear of the Lord. It's like a teenage driver who suddenly spots her father's car in her rearview mirror. Seeing him back there puts her on notice to be on her best behavior—to use her blinkers and stop at the yellow light, and to keep both hands on the wheel. But it also tells her that her father cares enough to follow her. It tells her that she's safe. Her father isn't trying to trap or trick her. He's trying to help her develop good habits; not just to be careful on this trip, but to obey the laws and stay safe until she gets home. She's driving on her own, but not completely on her own. So it is for the people of God. The fear of the Lord means we live life with our heavenly Father always in our rearview mirror. We glance up and see his brilliant holiness but also his care and love. Our response, the fear of the Lord, is a mix of reverence, trust, love, [and obedience]."

...because this applies to every person. [14] *For God will bring every act to judgment, every-thing which is hidden, whether it is good or evil* - The motive for fearing and obeying God here is the certainty of coming judgment. We can be eternally grateful as believers that the Savior has delivered us from a dread of being punished for our sins.

> "There is no fear in love; but perfect love casts out fear, because fear involves torment. But he who fears has not been made perfect in love" (1 Jn. 4:18).

We do not trust and obey because of a carnal cringing fear but because of a godly fear of displeasing God – which is in reality love. Through His finished work on Calvary, we have the assurance that we will never come into judgment for our sins, [though we can and will experience a loss of rewards] but have passed from death into life (John 5:24). Now we can say: There is no condemnation,

> There is no hell for me,
> The torment and the fire
> My eyes shall never see;
> For me there is no sentence,
> For me there is no sting
> Because the Lord who loves me
> Shall shield me with His wing. —*Paul Gerhardt*

So we have seen the Subject, Sermon, and the Summation.

I think Swindoll said it well:

"In the ragged-edge reality called earthly existence, life is somewhere between sad and bad. All it takes is a quick look around to discover why we line up to watch fantasies that take us to galaxies far, far away. Who wouldn't want to escape from an existence as boring and painful as ours? For many it's downright horrid. It's drug abuse. Its sleepless nights. Its headaches. Its heartaches. Its hate, rape, assault, jail sentences. Its sickness and sorrow. Its broken lives. Mainly as Solomon discovered long ago, its empty. There is nothing down here under the sun that will give you and me a sense of lasting satisfaction. It is planned that way! How else would we realize our need or the living God?"

Conclusion

§

THE BAD NEWS IS THAT Elvis has left the building, those of us who have listened to his music through the years miss anticipating a new song hitting the charts; but the good news is that God is not going anywhere! He is alive and well right here on planet earth. The main thing is to realize the day is coming when we, like Elvis, will also leave the building and go off into eternity. We need to prepare for that day, this very day by receiving the Lord Jesus Christ into our hearts as our personal Savior.

Let's begin with an honest evaluation of where we are. Allow me to ask a few simple questions. Have you come to a place in your life, where you know for certain that if you died you would go to heaven? The only answers to that question are, "Yes," or "No," or "I don't know." Take a moment and think about it.

GOD REALLY DOES LOVE YOU!

For God so loved the world [put your name here] that He gave His only begotten Son, that whoever believes in Him should not perish but have everlasting life." (John 3: 16 nkjv) It is natural to question this claim; we tend to wonder how God could love us with all of our problems and hang-ups. My wife and I have had several children. This may sound selfish, but when they were born they did nothing for us! For the first several months after they were born, they kept us up all hours of the night. We had to change their diapers and had to feed them. I think most of you know the routine. But we did love our children. Why? I suppose it was because we had something to do with them being in this world. They were our children; they even looked like us! You need to realize that God is the one who had everything to do with your coming into this world. Without God you would not even exist! He is the Creator and Sustainer of life. He created you in His image and loves you even though you have done nothing to deserve it.

So, What's a Fellow to Do?

Have you ever felt like your life lacked any significant purpose and meaning? Have these thoughts ever crossed your mind: "Where did I come from? Why am I here? Where am I going?" God knows the answer to those questions. He created you with a definite purpose in mind. The thief does not come except to steal, and to kill, and to destroy. I have come that they may have life, and that they may have it more abundantly. (John 10: 10) An abundant life is a life of purpose, meaning and fulfillment. That is what God offers you. This brings up an unavoidable question: what on earth happened" If God loves me and has this great purpose for my life, then why are both concepts so foreign to me? The answer is both profound and very simple.

Sin Separates!

You are a sinner. God's Word says, "For all have sinned and fall short of the glory of God" (Rom. 3: 23). You are a sinner by birth. God created Adam and Eve and put them in a garden with only one commandment. They were not to eat of a certain tree. They disobeyed God by taking a bite and thus they sinned. Now what kind of babies are two sinful people capable of having? The law of bio-genesis kicks in: like produces like. This is why there is no need to teach children how to tell a lie. We only need to teach them positive things like telling the truth. Ever notice how telling a lie just comes as natural as water falling off a duck's back? The reason for that is we are all born with a sin nature inherited from Adam. Therefore, just as through one man sin entered the world, and death through sin, and thus death spread to all men, because all sinned—" (Rom. 5: 12 nkjv) We are also sinners by behavior. Have you not sinned? The Bible commands us to love God with all our heart, mind, and soul. Have you always done that? Have you ever done that? Have you ever told a lie? Have you ever wanted to? God not only looks at our deeds but at our desires. The Bible clearly declares we have all sinned.

So What?

Here is the answer to that question. For the wages of sin is death, but the gift of God is eternal life in Christ Jesus our Lord. (Rom. 6: 23 nkjv) What you have earned from your sin is death. Death means separation. There is spiritual death— the separation of the spirit or soul from God. And the Lord God commanded the man, saying, "Of every tree of the garden you may freely eat; but of the tree of the knowledge of good and evil you shall not eat, for in the day that you eat of it you shall surely die. (Gen 2: 16-17 nkjv) The day they ate of it they did not physically die; that took place many years later. But God said "in the day" you eat of it you will die. They died spiritually that very day. There is also physical death— the separation of the spirit or soul from the body. And as it is appointed for men to die once, but after this the judgment ..." (Heb. 9: 27 nkjv) The fact that everybody dies physically is proof positive that everybody is spiritually dead. If we were not sinners we would not die. But, the statistics are rather impressive: one out of every one person dies! If you die physically, while you are spiritually dead, you will die eternally. Eternal death is the eternal separation of the spirit/ soul/ body from God's goodness, grace, mercy, and blessings. It is to be fully conscious and live in a place the Bible calls the lake of fire. Then Death and Hades were cast into the lake of fire. This is the second death. And anyone not found written in the Book of Life was cast into the lake of fire. (Rev. 20: 14-15 nkjv) Question: How can you say one moment, "God loves me," and then the next, "He condemns me"? Well, let's imagine you sitting on the bench in a judge's robe. Then the unthinkable happens. Your son whom you love very much is brought before you guilty of a capital offense. The penalty for his crime is the death penalty and the evidence is beyond clear as to his guilt. Would you sentence him to death? If you were a just judge you would; not because you no longer loved him, but in spite of your great love for him. God is holy, righteous, and just, as well as a God of love. This looks like bad news! But the very word gospel means good news, so where is this good news?

The good news is: Jesus Christ is God. Jesus Christ is God In the beginning was the Word, and the Word was with God, and the Word was God. (John 1: 1 nkjv) This is a great mystery, but the Bible teaches that God became God-man. And the Word became flesh and dwelt among us, and we beheld His glory, the glory as of the only begotten of the Father, full of grace and truth. (John 1: 14) Jesus Christ, The Substitute Jesus Christ is our substitute.

He lived a perfect life and then died in your place. But God demonstrates His own love toward us, in that while we were still sinners, Christ died for us. (Rom. 5: 8 nkjv) Let's put your judge robe back on for a minute. Imagine after sentencing your boy to be executed, you took off your robe, and then voluntarily offered to die in his place. That would make you just and loving at the same time. That is what Jesus Christ actually did for you. We do not understand all of this but must accept it by faith. I do not understand electricity, but I do not live in the dark. I do not understand how the digestive system works, but I still eat. I do not understand how a brown cow eats green grass, and produces white milk. You do not have to understand everything to be saved! Just that you are a sinner and that Jesus Christ died for your sin.

"HE IS NOT HERE, HE IS RISEN"

I am quite sure by now, you have heard plenty of Easter messages at church. Here is one more to add to your list. For I delivered to you first of all that which I also received: that Christ died for our sins according to the Scriptures, and that He was buried, and that He rose again the third day according to the Scriptures, and that He was seen by Cephas, then by the twelve. After that He was seen by over five hundred brethren at once, of whom the greater part remain to the present, but some have fallen asleep. (1 Cor. 15: 3-6) By rising from the dead He proved that He paid for all of our sins. If He hadn't, death would have held Him. It also proved that He had no sin of His own. If He had, He would have stayed dead like everyone else.

ONE WAY ONLY

We have all seen the "One Way Only" signs. That's the way it is with the way of salvation. There is only one person who can save. Jesus said to him, "I am the way, the truth, and the life. No one comes to the Father except through Me." (John 14: 6) You could line up every one of us on the West Coast with plans to swim to Hawaii. No doubt some would swim a lot farther than others, but we would all have one thing in common. Nobody would make it! It's impossible for anyone to swim from the West Coast to Hawaii. And it is more impossible for sinful man to make his way to a holy God on his own without experiencing God's wrath. To get from the West Coast to Hawaii by water, one needs a boat. The only salvation boat is the Lord Jesus Christ. That Jesus is the only way to be saved is as true as $2 + 2 = 4$. There is only one answer to that equation, and there is only one way to be saved. Nor is there salvation in any other, for there is no other name under heaven given among men by which we must be saved. (Acts 4: 12)

FACTS

These are only facts. Giving mental assent to these facts is not enough to save anyone. It is not enough just to intellectually give assent to these facts. We must believe and thus receive Christ. But as many as received Him, to them He gave the right to become children of God, to those who believe in His name. (John 1: 12) Facts must be wedded to faith, so what do we mean when we say believe, or place your faith in Christ? Faith involves the mind, the emotions and the will. I first heard Billy Graham on TV share this story of a tightrope walker named Charles Blondin who walked above Niagara Falls on a wire. He went back and forth. He even filled a wheelbarrow with bricks and took that across. A crowd gathered and Blondin asked them, "Do you believe I could put a man in this wheelbarrow and take him across?" The crowd all agreed he could. So, he turned to one man and asked, "Sir, will you be the first to get into the wheelbarrow? The man said, "No way!" You see, he didn't really believe. He believed in his mind that Blondin could take him across. He wanted him to in his emotions. But, he would not commit himself to Blondin and trust him to take him across. Saving faith involves our mind, emotion and will.

AMAZING GRACE

Most everyone is familiar with the song, Amazing Grace. We are saved by grace through faith in Jesus Christ. Now faith is not a work— faith is believing in the work of another. For by grace you have been saved through faith, and that not of yourselves; it is the gift of God, not of works, lest anyone should boast. (Eph. 2: 8-9) In D. James Kennedy's Truths That Transform, he quotes Dr. John H. Gerstner who says, "Christ has done everything necessary for his salvation. Nothing now stands between the sinner and God but the sinner's good works. Nothing can keep him from Christ but his delusion that he does not need Him— that he has good works of his own that can satisfy God. If men will only be convinced that they have no righteousness that is not as filthy rags; if men will see that there is none that does good, no, not one; if men will see that all are shut up under sin— then there will be nothing to prevent their everlasting salvation. All they need is need. All they must have is nothing. All that is required is acknowledged guilt.

But, alas, sinners cannot part from their virtues. They have none that are not imaginary, but they are real to them. So grace becomes unreal. The real grace of God they spurn in order to hold on to the illusory virtues of their own. Their eyes fixed on a mirage, they will not drink water. They die of thirst in the midst of an ocean of Grace."

Good Enough is Not Good Enough

The religious leaders of Jesus' day prayed three times a day, fasted twice a week, never missed going to the temple to worship, memorized the Old Testament (Luke 18: 9-12). And yet, Jesus said if you are not more righteous than they, you are not going to make it! For I say to you, that unless your righteousness exceeds the righteousness of the scribes and Pharisees, you will by no means enter the kingdom of heaven. (Matt. 5: 20 nkjv) Then Jesus says something rather startling. "Therefore you shall be perfect, just as your Father in heaven is perfect" (Matt. 5: 48 nkjv). Jesus said it takes perfect righteousness to get to heaven. We all know that nobody is perfect. How then can we be perfectly righteous before a perfectly righteous God? For He made Him who knew no sin to be sin for us, that we might become the righteousness of God in Him. (2 Cor. 5: 21 nkjv) The truth is there is only one person who ever lived a perfect life and that was Jesus Christ. The good news is, not only did Jesus die on the cross in our place to offer us forgiveness of all our sins, but He also offers us His perfect righteousness, placed on our account! The only sin Jesus ever knew was ours; the only righteousness we will ever know is His.

Never the Same!

Salvation is not an external thing. When you receive Jesus Christ as your Savior, He makes you a new creature within and the Holy Spirit takes up permanent residence within you. Therefore, if anyone is in Christ, he is a new creation; old things have passed away; behold, all things have become new. (2 Cor. 5: 17 nkjv) And because you are sons, God has sent forth the Spirit of His Son into your hearts, crying out, "Abba, Father!" (Gal. 4: 6) Thus you now have the desire (new nature) and the power (indwelling Holy Spirit) to live for God. You are positionally changed from being in Adam to now being in Christ. And you are experientially changed.

The inner transformation of regeneration and salvation begins the process of progressive sanctification, which ultimately leads to glorification. For it is God who works in you both to will and to do for His good pleasure. (Phil. 2: 13 nkjv) While we still have an old sin nature, and our enemy, Satan, opposes us every step of the way, and we must grow in the grace and knowledge of the Lord Jesus, it is also true that our entire life is different! If we are what we've always been, we not saved. I know that I am saved because on the 7th of May 1974 I received Jesus Christ as my Savior. And also because I have never gotten over it! And it is not that we are trying to be saved. If I asked you, "Are you an elephant?" You would not say, "Well, I'm trying to be!" You either are an elephant or you're not. No one who is trying to be saved understands salvation. You are either saved or you are not! You are saved because you have had a personal, life-changing life-changing encounter with Jesus Christ at a point in time. It is a matter of trusting, not trying.

So are you ready to be saved?

If this is something you want to do, then here is a suggested prayer. The words are not what's important, but your heart. If God is dealing with you, then cry out to God.

"Lord Jesus, I need you. Thank You for dying on the cross for my sins. I cannot save myself. I cannot even help you save me. But the best I know how, I confess that I am a sinner and believe, that the Lord Jesus Christ died on the cross for my sins and rose from the dead. I open the door of my life and receive you right now as my Savior. Come in and make me the kind of person you want me to be." If you just received Jesus Christ as your Savior— then you are saved! This promise is based on the authority of God's Word. But as many as received Him, to them He gave the right to become children of God, to those who believe in His name. (John 1: 12 nkjv)

Johnny A Palmer Jr.

www.ingramcontent.com/pod-product-compliance
Lightning Source LLC
Chambersburg PA
CBHW061720020426
42331CB00006B/1011